The
Web Wizard's
Guide to
Html

THE
WEB WIZARD'S
GUIDE TO
HTML

WENDY LEHNERT

Addison
Wesley

Boston San Francisco New York
London Toronto Sydney Tokyo Singapore Madrid
Mexico City Munich Paris Cape Town Hong Kong Montreal

Executive Editor: *Susan Hartman Sullivan*
Associate Editor: *Elinor Actipis*
Executive Marketing Manager: *Michael Hirsch*
Managing Editor: *Pat Mahtani*
Production Supervision: *Diane Freed*
Cover and Interior Designer: *Leslie Haimes*
Design Manager: *Regina Hagen*
Composition: *Gillian Hall, The Aardvark Group*
Copyeditor: *Jill Hobbs*
Proofreader: *Holly McLean-Aldis*
Manufacturing Coordinator: *Caroline Fell*

Access the latest information about Addison-Wesley titles from our World Wide Web site: *http://www.aw.com/cs*

Many of the designations used by manufacturers and sellers to distinguish their products are claimed as trademarks. Where those designations appear in this book, and Addison-Wesley was aware of a trademark claim, the designations have been printed in initial caps or all caps.

The programs and the applications presented in this book have been included for their instructional value. They have been tested with care but are not guaranteed for any particular purpose. The publisher does not offer any warranties or representations, nor does it accept any liabilities with respect to the programs or applications.

Library of Congress Cataloging-in-Publication Data
Lehnert, Wendy G.
      The Web wizard's guide to HTML / by Wendy Lehnert
          p. cm.
    Includes index.
    ISBN 0-201-74172-5 (alk. paper)
        1. HTML (Document markup language) I. Title.

QA76.76H94 L43 2002
005.7'2--dc21   2001034321

ISBN 0-201-74172-5

1 2 3 4 5 6 7 8 9 10—QWT—04030201

TABLE OF CONTENTS

PREFACE

About Addison-Wesley's Web Wizard Series

The beauty of the Web is that, with a little effort, anyone can harness its power to create sophisticated Web sites. Addison-Wesley's Web Wizard Series helps readers master the Web by presenting a concise introduction to one important Internet topic or technology in each book. The books start from square one and assume no prior experience with the technology being covered. Mastering the Web doesn't come with a wave of a magic wand; but by studying these accessible, highly visual textbooks, readers will be well on their way.

The series is written by instructors who are familiar with the challenges beginners face when learning the material. To this end, the Web Wizard books offer more than a cookbook approach: they emphasize principles and offer clear explanations, giving the reader a strong foundation of knowledge on which to build.

Numerous features highlight important points and aid in learning:

☆ Tips — important points to keep in mind

☆ Shortcuts — timesaving ideas

☆ Warnings — things to watch out for

☆ Review questions and hands-on exercises

☆ Online references — Web sites to visit to obtain more information

Supplementary materials for the books, including updates, additional examples, and source code, are available at `http://www.aw.com/webwizard`. Also available for qualified instructors adopting a book from the series are instructor's manuals, sample tests, and solutions. Please contact your Addison-Wesley sales representative for the instructor resources password.

About This Book

Mastery of Web design begins with the basics of Web page construction. Web page authors use a variety of tools to produce their creations, including HTML (the Hypertext Markup Language), graphics, and some very handy software utilities. HTML is the lingua franca of the Web, and all Web pages depend on HTML to organize and display everything from text to graphics and sound clips. But a Web page without graphics is rather dull and disappointing, so most Web page authors do a little work with graphics files as well as HTML files. There is also work behind the scenes: Web pages have to be properly installed on public Web servers for worldwide distribution, and hyperlinks have to be periodically tested in order to keep Web pages healthy and operational.

This book will teach you what you need to know to produce attractive Web pages for any Web site you want to build. Moreover, the foundation you get here will prepare you for the advanced techniques used by professional Web masters. If you've built Web pages using click-and-point programs like FrontPage, you may be surprised to discover that all you really need is a simple text editor. This book will show you how. And if you've never built a Web page at all, this book is the perfect place to start. Web page construction is easy and lots of fun as long as you don't get bogged down trying to learn every little detail. You'll create your first Web page in Chapter One, and each succeeding chapter will teach you how to make your Web pages more attractive, more useful, and easier to navigate. This book covers all of the most important fundamentals, and if you want to explore a topic in greater detail, you'll find valuable pointers to Web resources.

This book was inspired by the hundreds of undergraduates I've been privileged to teach at the University of Massachusetts at Amherst. Their endless enthusiasm for the Web prompted me to write this book, which is based on years of classroom experience and one-to-one help sessions. It has always a joy to teach when students want to learn. And although my students inspired me, my reviewers kept me focused and on target. I am truly grateful for their thoughtful feedback and excellent suggestions. Countless improvements and enhancements were based on ideas and observations so generously offered by these very knowledgeable reviewers: Fred Condo (California State University, Chico), Carla Gesell-Streeter (Cincinnati State Technical and Community College), David Lash, Donna L. Occhifinto (County College of Morris), and Ellen Taricani (Penn State University). Thank you, one and all. Last, but not least, I want to thank my daughter, Kate, who is quickly becoming an expert resource on Web design through her own ambitious explorations. In a few more years I may have a coauthor on my hands.

Wendy Lehnert
June 2001

CHAPTER ONE

WORLD WIDE WEB BASICS

The World Wide Web shows what can happen when millions of people go public with their thoughts and expertise on a global network. The Web is made of Web pages and behind each Web page is a Web page author. Some Web page authors are professional Web designers and some are young children who can barely type. You can become a Web page author, too. It's easy to create simple Web pages, and even easy-to-make Web pages can provide a lot of utility. In fact, you'll be pleasantly surprised to see how much you can accomplish with just a little effort.

Chapter Objectives

☆ Show how Web page authors and computers work together

☆ Look behind the scenes when a Web browser displays a Web page

☆ Explain what HTML is and how Web pages use HTML

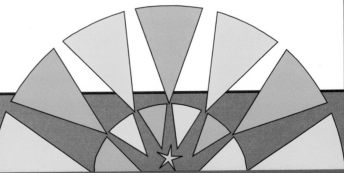

☆ Demonstrate how to create Web pages with nothing more than a text editor and a browser

☆ Explore the role of HTML standards on the Web

◎◎ The World Wide Web

The **World Wide Web** is a large collection of public documents—larger than the Library of Congress, and growing at a faster rate. The Web does not exist in any one place. Instead, it is distributed over a network of 10 million computers, each of which operates as a Web server. A **Web server** is a computer that stores documents and makes them available as Web pages through the Internet. A **Web site** is a collection of Web pages written by one Web page author (for a small site) or a team of Web page authors (for a large, professional site). A Web site can consist of a single Web page or thousands of Web pages.

Many Web sites require ongoing updates to keep their content timely and useful. A **Web master** is someone who maintains a Web site.

On the receiving end, people view Web pages with Web browsers. A **Web browser** is a computer program designed to retrieve documents from Web servers and display them on a computer monitor. To view a Web page, you need:

☆ An Internet-ready computer
(for example, with a telephone modem, cable modem, or networking card)

☆ An Internet access account
(for example, through your school, employer, or a commercial service provider)

☆ A Web browser
(for example, Microsoft Internet Explorer or Netscape Navigator)

You can also access the Web with handheld wireless devices and a variety of Internet appliances.

Whatever your hardware, the Web is most compelling as a visual medium. An appealing Web page presents useful content with color and style. Web pages routinely combine text and graphics, and they may also sport sound effects, music, animated art, or videos. When you create your own Web pages, you must decide which features will best convey the content for your particular Web site. To create your own Web site, you need the following items:

☆ An Internet-ready computer

☆ A text editor (or a special Web page construction program)

☆ An Internet access account

☆ A password-protected account on a Web server (usually included as part of your Internet access account)

Advanced Web page authors sometimes use specialized software for creating original computer graphics, audio files, or other multimedia elements for their Web sites. But a beginner can cover a lot of ground with nothing more than a simple text editor such as Notepad (if you run Windows) or SimpleText (if you are using a Mac).

Before you delve into the process of Web page creation, you need to understand a little more about the special partnership that exists between Web servers and Web browsers. In particular, you need to understand how Web pages connect to one another through the use of hyperlinks. A **hyperlink** (or just a **link)** is a clickable element on a Web page that directs the Web browser to a new Web page (or sometimes to a different location on the same Web page). Links allow users to jump from page to page to explore a single Web site or discover related Web sites. The act of moving through a collection of Web pages via a sequence of hyperlinks is called **browsing the Web** or **navigating a Web site**. Anyone can learn to browse the Web, but exactly what happens each time you position your mouse over a link and click it? The next section focuses on how Web pages move from Web servers to Web browsers and onto your computer monitor.

◎◎ Web Pages and Web Browsers

The World Wide Web is sometimes confused with the Internet, but it is really just one part of the Internet. The **Internet** (or simply the "Net") is a large global network consisting of thousands of smaller computer networks and millions of individual computers (see Figure 1.1).

We can think of the Internet in terms of all this hardware, or we can think of it in terms of the software that mediates computer communications on such a grand scale. A **communications protocol** is a set of rules that networked computers follow in order to share data and coordinate communications with one another. The World Wide Web obeys a communications protocol called the **HypertextTransfer Protocol (HTTP).** You may recognize the acronym HTTP from the Web page addresses that appear in your browser's location window. Each Web page is associated with a unique HTTP address, which makes it possible for browsers to retrieve that page from the Internet. A **Uniform Resource Locator (URL)** is another name for a Web page's HTTP address.

When you type a URL into a browser's location window and then press Return, the Web page associated with that URL appears in your browser's window. How does that happen?

When you ask your browser to return a URL, your browser examines the URL and pulls it apart into three pieces:

☆ A Web server name

☆ A directory path

☆ A filename

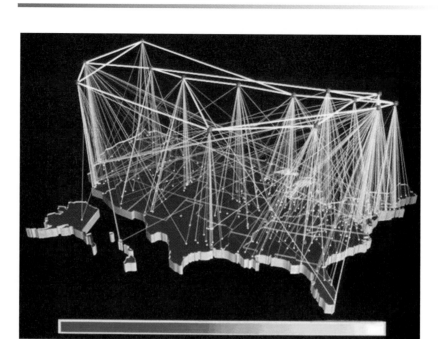

Figure 1.1 The Internet Connects Millions of Computers

Here's an example:

`http://www.nua.net/surveys/how_many_online/index.html`

| Web Server | Directory Path | Filename |

The browser is then ready to send a request out onto the Internet. It first contacts a special computer called a **domain name server (DNS)** and asks the DNS to translate the Web server's name into a numeric **Internet Protocol (IP)** address. Every computer with Internet access has a unique IP address, and all Internet communications rely on IP addresses. The request sent from the Web browser to the IP address tells the Web server at the specified IP address which Web page is being requested by identifying a directory path to the page as well as a filename for the page. The browser also sends a return address (another IP address) for its own computer, so that the Web server will know where to send the Web page. When the Web server receives this request, it finds the desired Web page and sends it back to the computer that requested it. A **file download** is a copy of a file that is transferred to a local computer from a remote computer. When a Web server sends a Web page back to a Web browser, we say that we have **downloaded** a Web page from a Web server.

The time it takes to complete a file download depends on the size of the file. The larger the file, the more time downloading it takes. We measure the speed of file

Web Pages and Web Browsers

☆**SHORTCUT** **Opening More Than One Browser Window**

Sometimes it is convenient to work with multiple browser windows. You can always open a new browser window whenever your browser is active. Many browsers will open a new browser window for you if you press ⌗Ctrl⌗-⌗N⌗ (or ⌗⌘⌗-⌗N⌗ on a Mac).

transfers over the Internet in terms of bandwidth consumption. **Bandwidth** is a ratio of memory units per second (for example, 28,800 bits per second). A computer may tap the Net over a low-bandwidth connection or a high-bandwidth connection. Low bandwidth results in slower file downloads, and higher bandwidth produces faster file downloads.

A browser can minimize its bandwidth consumption by keeping copies of recently downloaded Web pages on your computer's local hard drive. These Web pages are stored in a special section of the hard drive called the **browser's cache**. If the user later asks to see the same Web page a second time, the browser can retrieve that page from its cache instead of downloading it again from the Net. A Web page retrieved from the browser's cache consumes no bandwidth, and it can even be retrieved without an active Internet connection. Cache retrievals are much faster than file downloads over the Net.

☆**TIP** **To Cache or Not to Cache?**

Retrieving Web pages from a browser's cache is usually a good idea, because it minimizes bandwidth consumption and saves time. Sometimes, however, you may want to bypass the cache and make sure that you are viewing the most recent version of a specific Web page—one fresh from the server.

Your browser has preference settings that you can use to control when the browser accesses its cache and when it contacts the Web server. For Netscape Navigator, pull down the Edit menu and choose Preferences. Then expand the Advanced item in the navigation menu and choose Cache. For MSIE, pull down the Tools menu and choose Internet Options. Then make sure you're on the General tab and click the Settings button under Temporary Internet files.

The Files behind the Web Pages

Computer files come in a variety of formats, depending on the files' content. Files containing images use different file formats than do files containing typed text. Text files, sometimes called **ASCII text** files, are recognized as Web pages when they are named with the file extension `.html` or `.htm`. Although most Web pages are based on text files, Web browsers recognize many other file types. For example, `.gif` and `.jpg` indicate files containing images, and `.wav` and `.midi` denote files containing music or other sounds.

For now, we will focus on text files—the workhorses of the Web. Text files with `.html` (or `.htm`) extensions coordinate text and graphics in a browser's display window and support (optional) multimedia elements. We'll spend a lot of time learning about `.html` text files in Chapters Two and Three.

☆**TIP**   .html and .htm

When you create your Web pages, you should probably name your files with the .html file extension. The .htm variant is an artifact of older Microsoft software. Once upon a time, all files created under Microsoft Windows could only have file extensions containing a maximum of three characters. This restriction no longer applies to more recent versions of Windows, but you will still find Web pages that use the .htm extension.

You can initiate a file download from the Web in two ways:

☆ You can type a URL in the browser's location window.

☆ You can click a link on a Web page.

We've explained how URLs include three components that facilitate file downloads from a Web server. Entering a URL in a browser's location window and pressing the Enter key sends a request out onto the Internet for a Web page download. Clicking a link in a Web page initiates the exact same process. Each link on a Web page is associated with a URL. Indeed, you can see these hidden URLs if you look at the browser window's status bar when you position the mouse over the link (the status bar is usually found just inside the bottom edge of the browser window). Web page authors must specify server names, directory paths, and filenames for each link they add to a Web page. Links build bridges between Web pages. In fact, any Web page can link to any other Web page, as long as the correct address for the other Web page is known. In Chapter Four, we will see how links are added to Web pages.

Web Page Files and Web Page Displays

Every Web page author must understand that Web pages are fundamentally different from pages in books and magazines. When a book or magazine designer creates a printed page, the designer has total control over the final page display. He or she can fix the dimensions of the page and specify a particular typeface for the text.

The same is not true for Web page authors, however. Web pages are displayed by Web browsers, and browser users can control that page display to some extent. For example, users can resize the browser window to any dimensions desired. Users can even change the default typeface used by the Web browser by adjusting their browser preference settings. Other considerations come into play as well. Laptop users work with smaller browser display windows than do workstation users. Older users may prefer larger type than do younger users. Thus the Web page author faces a formidable challenge—to create a Web page that will look good to everyone despite many uncontrollable variables.

☆**SHORTCUT**   **Searching for Text on the Current Web Page**

If you are viewing a Web page with your browser, you can locate specific text strings within that page with your browser's text search feature. Go to the Edit Menu and select Find or Find in Page (or try the keyboard shortcut Ctrl-F). Enter your keyword or phrase in the pop-up window, and then click the Find Next button.

Happily, Web browsers have been designed to negotiate the best possible Web page display for individual users, no matter how they prefer to view their Web pages. To deal with windows that can be resized in any number of ways, your browser reworks each Web page to fill whatever space is available as best it can. Figure 1.2 shows how the same Web page is displayed differently depending on the dimensions of the browser window. You can see how this process works with your own browser. Visit a Web page with a lot of text and experiment by resizing your browser window. Watch how the page display changes as the size of your browser window becomes larger and smaller.

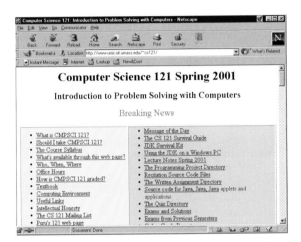 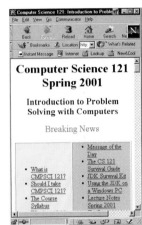

Figure 1.2 Browsers Control Their Own Web Page Displays

Because Web page authors do not have complete control over their own creations, they must be prepared to share some display decisions with the Web browsers that display their Web pages. No one can be expected to design Web pages that look great under all possible circumstances. For example, consider the challenge of designing attractive and effective Web pages for the little screens found on handheld computers. Nevertheless, Web page designers must understand that their pages will not look exactly alike to all the people viewing them.

◎◎ Using HTML to Control Web Page Displays

Although Web page authors do not have total control over how their pages appear to the user, they do have some control and can even make a few non-negotiable demands about how their Web pages should be displayed. Good Web page authors understand when to make such demands and when to allow for reasonable variations. To achieve this balance, they rely on the **Hypertext Markup Language (HTML).** With HTML, Web page authors can confidently insert formatting commands into their `.html` files, knowing that all HTML-compliant browsers will obey these commands in a specific way.

> ☆**TIP**   **WYSIWYG Web Page Construction Tools**
>
> Many software packages and Web sites are available for novice Web page authors that make it possible to create attractive Web pages without ever learning any HTML. So why bother to learn HTML? For fast results with a minimal learning curve, it's difficult to beat a good WYSIWYG (what you see is what you get) construction tool. Unfortunately, all of these tools have their limitations. If you want to create more than one or two Web pages, you may discover that WYSINWYW (what you see is not what you want). In such a case, you may need to make manual adjustments in the actual .html file behind your page.
>
> It's like buying a new car: You can order the make, model, and color easily enough. But no matter how nice the car seems when you drive it off the car dealer's lot, it will not be perfect until you add your personal music library, hang a dreamcatcher from the rear-view mirror, and maybe spring for customized seat covers. Likewise, when you need a particular feature or a special touch, you'll need to venture beyond the abilities of the WYSIWYG construction tools.

HTML Elements

An HTML element is a special block of text that conforms to strict syntactic requirements. When a Web browser recognizes an HTML element, it must display that element in accordance with an HTML standard. You can use an HTML element to add content to a Web page (as in the case of an image element), specify a style for a segment of text, or control the layout of text and images on a Web page. Many HTML elements exist, but you don't need to learn all of them before you start working on your first Web page. In fact, you can create some perfectly nice Web pages using just the HTML elements for line breaks, paragraph breaks, headings, and lists. These elements will all be covered in Chapter 2.

HTML elements are marked with special text strings called **HTML tags**. You add an HTML element to a text file by inserting an HTML tag or pair of tags with a text editor. For example, all proper .html files require a pair of tags that mark the beginning and the end of the file. The first tag, <html>, marks the beginning of the HTML element, and the second tag, </html>, marks the end of the element. Any HTML tag that starts with a forward slash (/) marks the end of an HTML element.

A Web browser will display any .html file, even if that file contains no HTML elements. Web browsers are designed to be forgiving about errors in Web page files, which is good news for Web page authors. Even so, a well-designed Web page should always contain a few basic page elements. Such elements help the Web browser render the Web page more efficiently, and they can be crucial for Web-related software other than Web browsers.

HTML tag pairs divide a Web page into segments containing different kinds of information. In addition, HTML tag pairs can be nested inside other tag pairs to produce a hierarchical structure for each Web page. Figure 1.3 shows a basic HTML template for a Web page. The indentation of text in this figure is not necessary, but it emphasizes the hierarchical structure of the HTML elements. The top level is represented by the main **HTML element**. Inside the HTML element are the **HEAD element** and the **BODY element**. The HEAD contains information that is useful behind the scenes, but which is not displayed as part of the Web page. For example, the **TITLE element** controls the browser window's title bar. The title bar is not part of the page display per se, so the `TITLE` element goes inside the `HEAD` element.

Although most HTML tags come in pairs, a few do not. Some elements, such as a line break, do not need to be terminated. Most basic HTML elements appear inside of the BODY portion of the Web page, which is where the visible elements of the Web page belong. Web browsers will recognize HTML tags typed in uppercase, lowercase, or mixed-case characters. Note, however, that some Web page markup languages currently under development (for example, XML and XHTML) do require tags to be in all lowercase characters. One of these markup languages may someday replace HTML, so it might be a good idea to get into the habit of typing lowercase tags now.

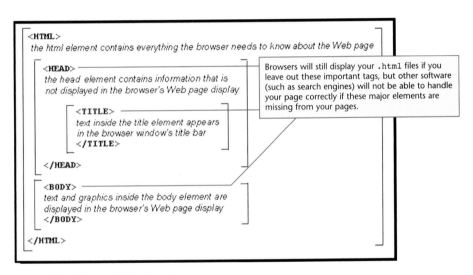

Figure 1.3 A General Web Page Template

Text Editors and HTML Editors

As noted earlier, all you need to create a Web page is a simple text editor—that is, HTML elements can be added to a text file using any text editor. If you use Windows, the best editor is Notepad. If you use the Mac, use SimpleText. You can use a more sophisticated editor, such as Microsoft Word (MS Word), but fewer opportunities for complications arise with a simple editor. Even with Notepad, a potential snag sometimes trips up beginners. When you try to open an existing `.htm` or `.html` file by using Notepad's directory dialog box, you must change the default file type setting from Text Documents to All Files (see Figure 1.4). If you leave the file type on its default value, no `.html` files will appear in the directory window.

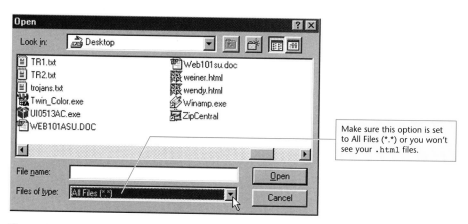

Figure 1.4 Adjust Notepad So That It Can See .html Files

Novice Web page designers who are familiar with MS Word often try to create their first Web page with this word-processing program. Unfortunately, Word can throw you off track when you try to edit `.html` files. Use Word if you must, but don't say we didn't warn you.

☆ **WARNING**   **Be Careful If You Use MS Word**

You can use MS Word to create a Web page file, but you should know some important things before you start. First, always save your file by using the Save As command on the File menu. Do not use the Save as HTML command in Word. This command invokes an HTML converter, which is not what you want when you are writing your own HTML files.

Second, when you use the Save As command, set the Save option to Text Only with Line Breaks (*.txt). If you do not change the default to this option, Word will not save your file as a plain text file and your browser will not be able to read the file.

Third, save your file with a filename that ends in `.html`. To do so, you must replace the default `.txt` extension in the filename window with an `.html` filename.

Fourth, MS Word may display a dialog box asking whether you really want to save your file in a text format (instead of the Word document format). You must answer Yes, even though the alert box makes it sound mildly dangerous.

Simple text editors force you to type each HTML tag in full. Although this process may seem tedious, it does help you learn the tag names. Once you have learned some HTML, you can speed up the process by using special software designed to expedite Web page development. Many Web page construction tools are available, including some designed specifically for beginners, and all are easy to use once you understand the basics.

Some HTML editors can preview your Web page as you edit it, which eliminates the need to switch back and forth between an editor and a browser. This speeds up the development cycle and makes it easier to experiment with different HTML elements while developing your page. If you plan to do a lot of Web page development, you will come to appreciate any time-saving features that accelerate the development process.

This book will not explain how to use a specific Web page construction kit, as we prefer to concentrate on learning the foundations of HTML. We strongly recommend the use of a simple text editor when you are first getting started. Once you've learned some HTML and become familiar with the Web page development cycle, you should then try out an HTML editor. Try downloading a freeware HTML editor from the Internet before you buy one in a box. If your interests in Web design are purely recreational, you may discover that all of your needs can be nicely met with the right freeware.

◎◎ Your First Web Page

Before we begin, make sure you have everything you need:

☆ A simple text editor (Notepad or SimpleText are best)

☆ A Web browser (any version of Internet Explorer or Netscape Navigator is fine)

For this exercise, you do *not* need:

☆ Internet access

☆ A password-protected account on a Web server

You will need Internet access and an account on a Web server only if you plan to publish your Web page so that the general public can see it. Chapter 8 will describe the process of publishing your Web pages. For now, we will concentrate on the process of creating and revising your Web pages. That can all be done offline, without access to the Internet.

☆TIP   Design versus Construction

An experienced Web page designer will do a lot of thinking and planning away from the keyboard before creating any files. The design phase of a Web site should always precede its construction phase. During the design phase, the author identifies the intended audience, outlines the site's intended content, plans the overall organization of the site, and possibly marks up storyboards (especially if the site will include extensive graphics).

This book does not address the stages of the design process, but if you are serious about building the best possible Web site, you will want to read up on the process of Web site design.

Step 1: Create a File Named firstpage.html

Using your text editor, type in the following text:

```
<html>
<head>
<title>My First Web Page</title>
</head>
<body>
<p>This is my first Web page.</p>
</body>
</html>
```

After you have entered this text, save it under the filename `firstpage.html`. It doesn't matter where you save the file, as long as you can find it again. Some people like to save work-in-progress on the desktop so they can readily find it again. Note that we have inserted a **paragraph element** inside the body with the <p></p> tag-pair. This element organizes the text inside its tag-pair as a visible text block offset by a blank line, so as to separate it from any surrounding text. The effects of the paragraph element will become more apparent when we add more text to our Web page.

Step 2: View firstpage.html with Your Browser

Next, we will load `firstpage.html` into your Web browser. You have two convenient ways to do this. If you have the icon for the `firstpage.html` file in view, double-click the file icon. Alternatively, if your browser window is active, pull down the File menu and choose the Open or Open Page command. Although each browser is slightly different, all browsers will give you an opportunity to open a local `.html` file from your own hard drive. You can easily direct your browser to a local file by navigating your way to the file and selecting it inside a dialog box. Look for a Browse button or a Choose File button to specify the location of your file by selecting it (see Figure 1.5).

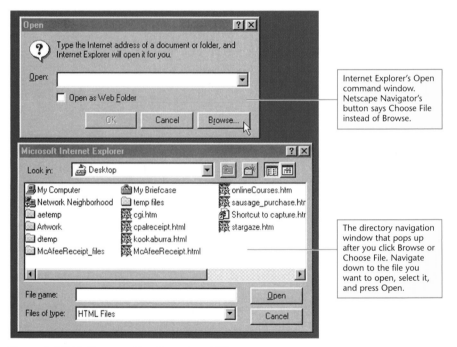

Figure 1.5 Web Browsers Can Open Local Files

When you view `firstpage.html` with your browser, you should see the title in the browser's title bar. Only the text inside the BODY element will be visible in the browser's Web page display. To review the source code for your page, return to your text editor or pull down your browser's View menu and then select Page Source. Your browser will then display the underlying `.html` file, sometimes with color-coded HTML tags to help you sort out the various HTML elements.

> **☆TIP** **Viewing the Source Code for a Web Page on the Web**
>
> Whenever you are viewing a Web page with your browser, you can go to the View menu and select Page Source to look at the HTML code behind the page. This strategy is an honorable way to learn HTML. If you see something you like on a Web page, examine the source file behind the page to see how the page author accomplished it. Don't be dismayed if some source files are beyond your comprehension—you can still learn from the ones that are within your reach.

Step 3: Modify firstpage.html with Your Editor

Activate your text editor and make some changes to `firstpage.html`. For example, add some new text to the `BODY` element, and experiment with blank lines or empty spaces. Note that these changes will not be visible to your browser immediately. To see your new modifications, you must do two things:

1. Save your changes (select Save on the File menu).

2. Reload your Web page (use a Reload or Refresh button, or press `Ctrl`-`R`).

Each time you modify your `.html` file, you will need to do this little two-step dance to see the effects of your changes.

> **☆WARNING** **Don't Forget to Save Your Changes**
>
> Many beginners get confused when they make a change to their .html file and then they can't see the effects of that change after reloading the page into the browser. If you forget to save your file before reloading, your browser will reload the file, but it will be the old version of the file without the newest changes.

The Web Page Development Cycle

When you create Web pages from scratch, you can't expect them to be perfect the first time you view them with your browser. The process of Web page development involves many repetitions of a four-step cycle, with each iteration bent on making your page look exactly the way you want:

The Four-Step Development Cycle

1. Save your file with the Save command.

2. Load the file into your Web browser.

3. Review the Web page to see how it looks in the browser.

4. Revise your page as needed using a text editor or an HTML editor.
   (Go back to Step 1.)

The development cycle begins with a first-pass attempt at a Web page in a text editor. Make sure to save your new file with an `.html` or `.htm` file extension.

Be careful to remember Steps 1 and 2, or your browser will not display your last round of page revisions. It can be easy to forget step 1 if you become preoccupied with a troublesome HTML element. If you ever find yourself looking at the exact same Web page display when your last round of changes should have made a visible difference, go back to your editor and resave the file—even if you feel confident that you saved it before. Then return to your browser and reload the file. If the page still looks the same, then your edits just didn't have the expected effect.

☆SHORTCUT   Review Your Web Page Edits Early and Often

It is a good idea to make only a few changes during each iteration of the development cycle. That way you can isolate any changes that produce unexpected results. When difficulties arise, you'll find it very helpful to know which edits are responsible for which changes. If you make too many changes at once, it becomes more difficult to zero in on those causing problems. In the long run, you'll save time by making more short trips around the development cycle, rather than fewer, but longer passes.

☆TIP   You Could Read Chapter Eight Now

Once you've viewed your first Web page with a Web browser, you are well on your way to becoming a bona fide Web page author. First, however, you need to publish a Web page on a Web server. This task is accomplished by uploading your .html file(s) to a Web server. Uploading files is simple once you've mastered the details, but beginners sometimes need to practice this crucial step.

To get a head start on the publishing part of the process, jump ahead to Chapter Eight and try installing your first Web page on a public Web server. If you prefer to explore HTML in more detail first, you can put off publishing for a little longer. Just remember, you can tackle Chapter 8 at any time, and you probably shouldn't wait until after Chapter Seven.

◎◎ Industry Standards and the Web

The Internet has been characterized as a lawless frontier without rules or leadership. This portrayal has been used to describe the behavior of some people online, but it couldn't be further from the truth in regard to the software that makes the World Wide Web work. All Web servers and browsers must recognize and obey the rules of the Hypertext Transfer Protocol (HTTP), and all Web page authors must work within the constraints of the Hypertext Markup Language (HTML). You cannot hope to make millions of computers interact predictably and reliably without a common language and some agreement about how that language should be modified when necessary. These agreements are realized by the adoption of industry standards—that is, standards for Web servers, standards for Web browsers, and standards for Web page authors.

The most important standards for Web page authors dictate how a Web browser should render its Web pages. If each browser applied its own display standards, the Web would soon fall apart. Most people know about Netscape Navigator and Internet Explorer, but more than 100 different Web browsers exist—and anyone can write another browser. To hold it all together, the community of Web programmers, Web technicians, and Web page designers has bestowed the **World Wide Web Consortium (W3C)** with the authority to set industry standards for Web page authors. In particular, the W3C establishes and announces new standards for HTML.

Sometimes the programmers behind a leading Web browser will try to influence the thinking of the W3C by implementing an unauthorized HTML extension. A **browser-specific extension** is an HTML tag or tag feature that is recognized by at least one Web browser, but not by the W3C. If enough Web page authors begin using the extension, it might materialize as part of the next official HTML standard. Alternatively, the extension might never be accepted by the W3C, in which case the extension remains a browser-specific deviation from the industry standard.

☆WARNING **Deviations from the Standard**

Although using the Page Source command with random Web pages might be an honorable way to learn HTML, it is always a good idea to find out whether you are learning a trick that's part of the official HTML standard. If you don't check the standard, you might inadvertently adopt a browser-specific extension that works with only one particular browser.

Internet Explorer uses one set of HTML extensions, and Netscape Navigator employs a different set of HTML extensions. If you use an Internet Explorer extension in the HTML code for a Web page, that Web page will look fine under Internet Explorer, but will have a different appearance when viewed in Netscape Navigator. You may have noticed that some Web sites post a little warning near the top of their home pages: "This page looks best when viewed by Netscape Navigator" or "Best viewed with Internet Explorer." These notices are not just idle announcements intended to promote the author's favorite Web browser. When you see such a notice, you are probably visiting a Web page that uses browser-specific extensions.

Over the years, the HTML standard has evolved, and Web browsers have likewise evolved to keep pace. The current W3C HTML standard is HTML 4.01 (released in December 1999). You can use a variety of tools to ensure that your Web pages comply with this standard.

An HTML validation service on the Web (see the online resources at the end of this chapter) will analyze your HTML code and generate a report that pinpoints errors in your file. Note that most Web pages written by hand will contain HTML errors. Because Web browsers work hard to display Web pages despite their errors, many such HTML flaws will not hurt your Web page display. As a result, you might wonder whether it's really necessary to use a validation service to detect HTML errors. Error correction can be a time-consuming and difficult process, especially for someone who is still learning HTML.

☆TIP **Using a Validation Service**

Most validation services want to know which version of HTML your Web page should be checked against. You can tell them by inserting an extra line of documentation at the very beginning of your .html file. If you want to comply with HTML 4.01, insert the following SGML tag (yet another markup language) at the beginning of your file:

```
<!DOCTYPE HTML PUBLIC "-//W3C/DTD HTML 4.01//EN">
```

This DTD (Document Type Definition) statement provides useful information not just to validation services, but also to any browser that is ready and able to interpret your document according to this DTD.

A better approach is to minimize the number of errors in your Web page in the first place. HTML editors watch for errors as they happen and attempt to prevent their inclusion. For example, if you open a new file using an HTML editor named **HTML-Kit** (see Figure 1.6), it will automatically fill in the tags for the Web page template shown in Figure 1.3 (in addition to providing a DTD statement identifying the HTML standard used by the editor).

In Figure 1.6, the HTML tags appear in blue for easy reading. The HTML editor also allows you to add new tags by clicking buttons on toolbars instead of typing them in. The buttons ensure that the tag names will not include typos, and that each tag has an appropriate termination tag (if necessary).

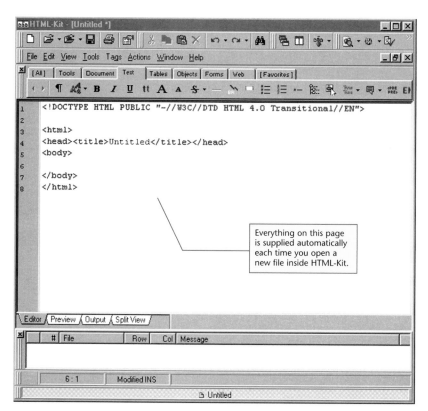

Figure 1.6 HTML Editors Help Web Page Authors Produce Correct HTML

If Web page construction becomes part of your daily routine, you may find that special HTML editors and other construction tools can keep your Web pages in sync with the latest HTML standard. They may also prevent Web page errors that may be difficult to later track down and fix.

☆ Summary

▷ The World Wide Web relies on 10 million Web servers to deliver Web pages to Web browsers on demand.

▷ Web browsers determine which files to download from which Web servers by examining addresses encoded in URLs.

▷ Web page authors control Web page displays by adding HTML tags to text files.

▷ You can design Web pages by using nothing more than a simple text editor and a Web browser.

▷ All Web page authors should know which HTML elements are part of the accepted HTML standard and which are browser-specific extensions.

☆ Online References

HTML Goodies (lots of good tutorials for beginners)
`http://htmlgoodies.earthweb.com/`

Web Design Group (a friendly HTML resource for beginners)
`http://www.htmlhelp.com/`

WebMonkey (an online magazine for beginners and beyond)
`http://www.webmonkey.com/`

HTML Design I (a comprehensive clearinghouse for online resources)
`http://www.devs.com/zresources/html.html`

HTML Editors and Associated Tools (mostly for Windows)
`http://webdevelopersjournal.com/software/html_editors.html`

Top HTML Editors for the Mac (suitable for both beginners and professionals)
`http://macworld.zdnet.com/netsmart/features/editorintro.html`

HyperText Markup Language Home Page (from the W3C)
`http://www.w3.org/MarkUp`

HTML Validation Service
`http://validator.w3.org/file-upload.html`

☆ Review Questions

1. What is the Hypertext Transfer Protocol (HTTP) and how is it used by Web browsers?

2. What three types of information are found in a Web page's URL?

3. What is a Web browser cache and how is it beneficial?

4. How do Web page layouts differ from page layouts in books and magazines?

5. Name the four HTML tags that form the basis for a Web page template.

6. Why is it better for beginners to work with a simple text editor instead of an HTML editor or Web page construction kit?

7. Describe two ways to open a local `.html` file (a file on your hard drive) with your browser.

8. How can you view the source file for someone else's Web page?

9. Describe each step in the four-step Web page development cycle.

10. What is a browser-specific extension? How can you make sure that your own Web pages do not include any browser-specific extensions?

☆ Hands-On Exercises

1. Try to reconstruct the basic HTML template for a Web page from memory. If you get stuck, consult Figure 1.3.

2. Visit `http://www.w3.org/People/Raggett/tidy/` and examine the source file for this Web page. Look at the first line and compare it with the first line of the file shown in Figure 1.6. How do the two lines differ?

3. Visit an HTML tutorial by Joe Burns at `http://htmlgoodies .earthweb.com/primers/primer_7.html`. Perform a text search (search for a text string on just this one Web page) for the word "popular" (don't include the quotes) to read about free Web page services. What are the two most popular free Web server sites? Why do some people dislike these free services? (Consult the shortcut box on page 6 if you aren't sure how to conduct a text search on a Web page.)

4. Create an `.html` file with a text editor. Put your name and address in the BODY element, so that this information will be visible when you view your page with the browser. Save the file and open it from inside your Web browser. How does your name and address look in your text editor? How does it look in the browser's display? Can you explain any differences that you see?

5. Create an `.html` file with a text editor. Type the following text inside the BODY element:

```
The name "Chicago" means "onion" <in
the language of the Pottawatomies> or
possibly "stinking onion" depending
on what you read.
```

Now view your file with a Web browser. Do you notice anything interesting about your Web page display? Can you explain this?

CHAPTER TWO

BASIC TEXT FORMATTING

Most Web pages use text as their primary means of communication. Providing quality content should always be your first priority when you add text to any Web page. But the visual presentation of text on a Web page can greatly enhance or detract from the underlying content. Which font should you use? How large should it be? What color type against what color background is best? Most book authors do not participate in design process associated with book production. Traditionally, authors produce the words, and then graphic designers take over from there. Web page authors, however, must do it all: they not only write their text, but must also figure out how to display those words on the Web. On the Web, even words require a visual flair.

Chapter Objectives

☆ Show how to create headings and paragraphs for Web pages

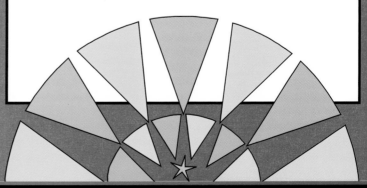

☆ Explain how to control a variety of features associated with text

☆ Learn how to add three types of lists to a Web page

☆ Explore layout and white-space controls for blocks of text

◎◎ Headings, Paragraphs, and Horizontal Rules

It's a good idea to tell the reader about the subject of your document before diving into a lot of text explaining that topic in detail. Paper-based documents use titles for this purpose. In Chapter One, you saw how an HTML element named `TITLE` is used to place identifying information in the title bar for the browser window. If you want to insert a title inside the browser's window, at the top of your Web page display, you must add a different element to your `BODY` element—the **HEADING element** (also known as a **HEADER element**).

The `HEADING` element should not be confused with the `HEAD` element—these elements are very different things. Happily, the HTML tags for the `HEAD` element and the `HEADING` elements are easier to distinguish than the terms *head* and *heading*. As noted in Chapter One, the tag-pair for the `HEAD` element is `<head></head>`. In contrast, the tag-pairs for the `HEADING` elements come in six varieties:

```
<h1></h1>
<h2></h2>
<h3></h3>
<h4></h4>
<h5></h5>
<h6></h6>
```

These `HEADING` elements are used to signal the hierarchical structure of an online document, much as chapter titles and section subtitles indicate the hierarchical structure in a book. Use `H1` for the top-level title, `H2` for the next-level title, and so on. Most documents can be handled adequately with `H1`, `H2`, and `H3`; few will require `H5` or `H6` headings.

The HTML standard merely states that headings with smaller numbers should be displayed more prominently than headings with larger numbers. In practice, browsers display the six headings in six sizes, ranging from very large (for `H1`) to very small (for `H6`). All are rendered in boldface to distinguish them from ordinary text.

You can place a heading anywhere inside the `BODY` of a Web page, and you can insert as many headings as you want. Be careful when using the least prominent `HEADING` elements: they produce very small text and should be reserved for items that need to appear in fine print. Figure 2.1 illustrates the use of the six `HEADING` elements and the tags that create them.

☆ **TIP** **Add Comments to Your Source Files**

Comments are text segments that become visible only when you view the source file for the Web page—they are never displayed by Web browsers. You use comments to annotate specific portions of your Web page. They will help you get oriented when you need to revise or update a Web page that you haven't reviewed in a long time, and they will prove invaluable if someone else needs to revise your Web page. Comments must be placed inside a comment tag, which starts with an exclamation mark and two hyphens, and ends with two hyphens right before the closing angle bracket.

```
<!-- (put your comment here) -->
```

```
<h1>Computer Science 100</h1>
<!-- use H1 for titles at the top
of a Web page -->

<h2>An Introduction to Computer
Programming</h2>
<!-- use H2 for subtitles or
chapter titles -->

This course presents basic
concepts in computer programming.
Students will learn to program
in Java, a modern object-oriented
programming language.

<h3>Who Should Take 100?</h3>
<!-- use H3 for section heads -->

This is a required course for
computer science majors. Non-
majors are welcome but should
understand that 100 is fast-paced and time-consuming.

<h4>Prerequisites</h4>
<!-- use H4 for section heads -->

Math 100 (basic math)

<h5>3 Credits</h5>
<!-- use H5 for "fine print" -->

<h6>No Pass/Fail Option</h6>
<!-- use H6 for "very fine print" -->
```

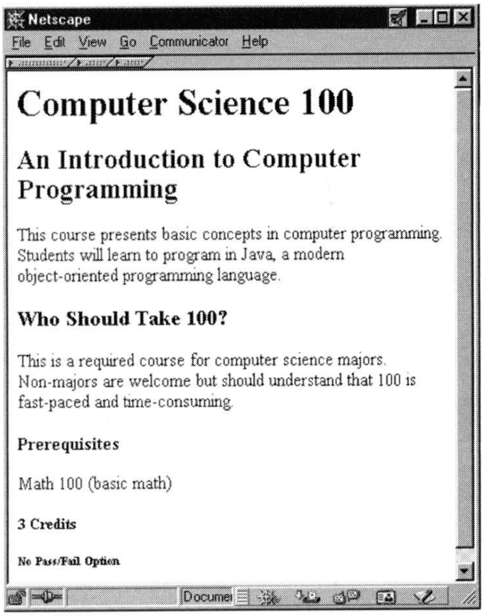

Netscape — File Edit View Go Communicator Help

Computer Science 100

An Introduction to Computer Programming

This course presents basic concepts in computer programming. Students will learn to program in Java, a modern object-oriented programming language.

Who Should Take 100?

This is a required course for computer science majors. Non-majors are welcome but should understand that 100 is fast-paced and time-consuming.

Prerequisites

Math 100 (basic math)

3 Credits

No Pass/Fail Option

Figure 2.1 The Six HEADING Elements

HEADING elements do more than change the size of the text enclosed in the tag-pairs. Most browsers display headings in boldface, and they insert blank lines before and after each heading (see Figure 2.1). Headings can also be placed on a Web page in different ways through the use of **attributes**. Adding specific attributes to an HTML element enables you to fine-tune that element. For example, you might want to center a heading instead of having it appear left-justified. An **HTML attribute** is a property of an HTML element, and each attribute consists of an **attribute name** and an **attribute value**.

Even if you don't add your own attributes to an HTML element, your browser will assume default values for specific attributes. For example, the HEADING elements in Figure 2.1 are all left-justified because no alignment attribute was specified inside the HEADING tags. That's because the default alignment for HEADING elements is left justification. You can always override this default alignment if you prefer something different, by simply including your own alignment attribute inside the H1 tag. In Figure 2.2, the attribute name ALIGN and the attribute value CENTER have been added to the H1 element, producing a centered heading.

```
<html>
<head>
<title> The Dachshund
</title>
<body>
<h1 align="center">
The Dachshund</h1>
<p> The dachshund was
originally used to hunt
badgers, wild boar,
foxes, and rabbits.
</body>
</html>
```

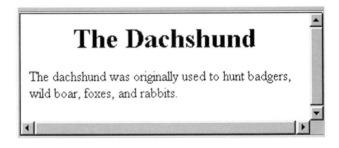

Figure 2.2 A Centered Heading

Much of the fine-tuning that goes into a Web page involves setting attribute values inside HTML elements. A good HTML reference (see the URL list at the end of this chapter) will describe the many attributes and attribute values that can be inserted into HTML elements. Although this book does not provide a comprehensive review of all available attributes (or all HTML tags, for that matter), it does describe the most useful ones.

☆**WARNING** **Tag Attributes and Attribute Values**

When you add attributes to an HTML tag, make sure that each attribute goes inside the angle brackets of the leading tag (the first tag in a start/stop pair). If an attribute appears outside the angle brackets, the browser will not recognize it. You should also put all attribute values inside a pair of double quotes. Although a browser may recognize some attribute values without the double quotes, it may ignore these unquoted values in other cases. Attribute values, like tag names, can appear in either uppercase or lowercase, although lowercase is preferred (casting an eye toward XML and XHTML).

Headings break long text documents into useful subsections. Shorter subsections are easier to digest than long, undifferentiated blocks of text, and well-placed headings help readers keep track of the bigger picture. At a lower level, paragraphs serve a similar purpose.

A well-written paragraph develops one main point, and a paragraph break tells the reader to shift gears as the author moves from one idea to the next. The **paragraph element** signals the beginning of a paragraph. Most browsers insert a blank line before the paragraph element, thereby signaling the start of a new paragraph. To mark paragraphs in your `.html` file, insert the tag-pair `<p></p>` at the beginning and end of each paragraph. You won't see an indentation on the first line of the paragraph, but the blank line works well enough as a paragraph signal (see Figure 2.3). To insert the equivalent of a carriage return without getting the blank line associated with a new paragraph, you can include a **line break element**, `<br>`.

As noted earlier, paragraph elements break up text at a low level, and heading elements break up text at a higher level with titles. If you want to achieve something in between, try experimenting with the **horizontal rule element**. To emphasize a break in the text without titles or subtitles, insert an `<hr>` tag. This tag produces a horizontal line across the page (see Figure 2.3). You can also insert horizontal rules immediately before a heading element to achieve additional emphasis.

Whenever you encounter a new HTML element, you should investigate the available attributes for that element. As Figure 2.3 demonstrates, attributes for the horizontal rule element can be used to align the rule and control its width within the browser window. Additional attributes control the size (thickness) of the rule and whether it should be displayed as a 3-D (shaded) element or a 2-D (flat) element. Paragraph alignment can be used to right-justify text in case you want to set a line of text to the right of your document (for example, a date or an e-mail address). Table 2.1 summarizes the most commonly used paragraph and horizontal rule attributes.

☆**TIP**   **What if I Leave Out the `</p>` Tag?**

According to current HTML standards, the `</p>` is optional. You can probably tell if a Web page was written with an HTML editor or by hand by checking for `</p>` tags (HTML editors always insert them, whereas people writing HTML by hand usually cut corners and leave them out). Note that if you ever need to make the transition from HTML to XML or XHTML, both of those markup languages require the `</p>` tag for their paragraph elements. If you get into the habit of closing all your paragraphs now, you may have less of an adjustment to make later.

```
<html>
<head>
<title> The Dachshund
</title>
<body>
<h1 align="center">The
Dachshund</h1>
<p> The dachshund was origi-
nally used to hunt badgers,
wild boar, foxes, and rab-
bits.
</p>
<hr align="center"
width="50%">
<p>
The name "dachshund" means
"badger dog" in German,
where these dogs were first
bred. Woodcuts and paintings
from the fifteenth century
show badgers being hunted by
dogs with short legs, long
bodies, and hound-like ears.
</p>
<p>
To this day, the dachshund's short muscular legs are well suited
for burrowing into tunnels and underground lairs, although the
breed has never been active as a hunting dog in the United
States. As pets, dachshunds are lively, loyal, and assertive
watchdogs.
</p>
</body>
</html>
```

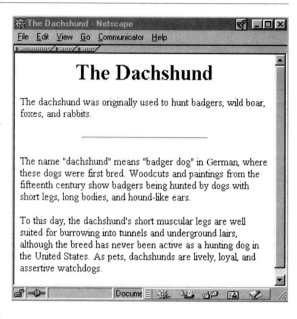

Figure 2.3 The Paragraph and Horizontal Rule Elements Make Text Easier to Read

Table 2.1   Selected Text Organization Elements

HTML Element	Attributes	Attribute Values	What the Attribute Does
`<h1></h1>` (heading) `<h2></h2>` (heading) `<h3></h3>` (heading) `<h4></h4>` (heading) `<h5></h5>` (heading) `<h6></h6>` (heading)	`align=`	`left`, `center`, `right`	Alignment justifies or centers the heading. The default alignment is left justification.
`<p></p>` (paragraph)	`align=`	`left`, `center`, `right`	Alignment is used to justify or center the text and can also be used to manipulate single lines of text.
` `	`clear=`	`left`, `right`	These attributes are only used in conjunction with images and tables (see Chapter 3).
`<hr>`	`align=`	`left`, `center`, `right`	Alignment is used to justify or center the horizontal rule. The default alignment is centered.
	`noshade`	[*takes no value*]	Eliminates the default 3-D effect.
	`size=`	`n` (an integer)	Sets the thickness of the rule in pixels. The default size is 2 pixels.
	`width=`	`n` (an integer) or `n%`	An integer value sets the width of the horizontal rule in pixels. A percentage value sets the width as a percentage of the browser window's width. The default width is 100%.

◎◎ Working with Type Fonts and Type Styles

Text displays mean working with choices for your text. Text can be displayed with different type faces (for example, sans serif or cursive), styles (for example, italic or boldface), and sizes (for example, 10-point or 14-point). Although computer displays may give you all the options available to a traditional publishing operation, you must use extra care when designing Web pages that contain text. Understanding how to make good choices for your text displays is crucial so that your Web pages will look good to everyone who views them.

If you use a sophisticated word-processing program, you are probably accustomed to working with a large selection of **type faces** (sometimes called **type fonts**) for your documents. Unfortunately, type font selections are somewhat problematic in HTML, because the standard does not specify a set of core fonts that must be shared by all HTML-compliant computers. Different computers come with different preinstalled type fonts. Even when the same font is available on two computers, it might be known by different names. To make matters even worse, browser users who have a preference for a specific type face can configure their browsers to override the font specifications of a Web page author. Consequently, even when your first-choice font is available, you can't be certain that this font will be used to display your Web pages. Instead, you must try to second-guess what is likely to happen to your Web pages as they are displayed on different computers with different type font libraries.

Font choices are controlled by the **font element** and the values you assign to its **face attribute**. The FACE attribute can be given multiple attribute values, which in turn gives you maximal flexibility. When the FACE attribute is assigned a list of possible values, a browser works through the list from left to right, selecting the first font in the list that is available on that particular machine. If you stick to common fonts and are careful to include the fonts found on the most popular computer platforms, you should be able to control the fonts seen on your Web pages (at least as much as possible).

The standard font option groups listed below are the safest choices for the FONT FACE attribute. Note that each font option in these font groups produces exactly the same type font—the same font just goes by different names on different computer platforms.

Standard Font Option Groups (Absolutely Safe Text Fonts)

For a sans serif font, list three options:

Arial (for Windows)
Geneva (for Macs)
Helvetica (for all others)

<font face="Arial, Geneva, Helvetica">
This is what Arial/Geneva/Helvetica looks like.

For a serif font, list two options:

Times New Roman (for Windows)
Times (for Macs)

<font face="Times New Roman, Times">
This is what Times New Roman/Times looks like.
(Times New Roman is the default font for most browsers.)

For a monospaced font, list two options:

Courier New (for Windows)
Courier (for Macs)

```
<font face="Courier New, Courier">
This is what Courier New/Courier looks like.
```

As part of an effort to expand the set of fonts commonly available on all platforms, a free set of fonts called Core Web Fonts has been designed for use on the Web and is available for both Windows and Macintosh computers. Although these fonts have become increasingly common on Windows and Macintosh computers, some people viewing your Web page probably won't have all of these options in their font library. If you use one of these fonts on a Web page, back it up with one of the safe options listed above—just in case. The Core Web Fonts are listed below.

Core Web Fonts (Somewhat Risky Text Fonts)

Andale Mono – This is what Andale Mono looks like.

Arial – This is what Arial looks like.

Arial Black – **This is what Arial Black looks like.**

Comic Sans MS – This is what Comic Sans MS looks like.

Courier New – This is what Courier New looks like.

Georgia – This is what Georgia looks like.

Impact – **This is what Impact looks like.**

Times New Roman – This is what Times New Roman looks like.

Trebuchet MS – This is what Trebuchet MS looks like.

Verdana – This is what Verdana looks like.

As noted earlier, Web page authors must ultimately bow to the preferences of individual readers. Someone with poor vision might set his or her browser preference to display an easy-to-read font; that preference will then override any FONT FACE values specified by the Web page author. For this reason, it is not wise to design a page that depends too heavily on specific type face properties.

Two other useful FONT attributes are COLOR and SIZE. To change the color of your text, set the COLOR attribute to one of the following standard color names: aqua, black, blue, fuchsia, gray, green, lime, maroon, navy, olive, purple, red, silver, teal, white, or yellow. Internet Explorer and Netscape Navigator also recognize hundreds of other color names (the list of URLs at the end of this chapter includes a site that lists all of them). Alternatively, you can specify a color using a hexadecimal color code (see Chapter Three).

To change the size of your type, you can reset the size attribute to any integer value between 1 and 7 (the default value is 3). Alternatively, you can adjust the font size relative to the current size by providing values of the form +n (to make it n points larger) or –n (to make it n points smaller).

Now that you are familiar with the FONT element, you should understand that this tag is a *deprecated* tag according to the most recent HTML standards. **Deprecated tags** and **deprecated tag attributes** remain part of the official HTML standard and will be recognized by HTML-compliant browsers for some time to come, but the W3C discourages their use. In most cases, **Cascading Style Sheets (CSS)** are considered a better option. The W3C encourages the use of CSS in order to separate document organization from document display. The idea is to restrict HTML to organizational elements (for example, using HTML's `HEADING` elements to mark document segments) and use CSS for controls that address specific display properties associated with the document (for example, to control font sizes and type face selections). If the display properties of a document are neatly segregated from the rest of the document, the document can be more easily adapted to different online environments. This book does not cover CSS, but you can learn about it on the Web (see the URL list at the end of this chapter).

☆ **TIP**   **Why Learn Deprecated Tags and Tag Attributes?**

Many of the HTML tags and tag attributes described in this book are deprecated. (For example, the `FONT` element and all of the `HR` attributes listed in Table 2.1 are deprecated). Why pay attention to these doomed tags? It's a good question. The answer is twofold: (1) The deprecated HTML tags and tag attributes will persist for years to come (browsers like to be "backward compatible), and (2) the older HTML standards offer a path of least resistance for beginners. If you intend to pursue HTML professionally, you should learn CSS just as soon as you finish this book. If your interest in Web page design is more recreational than professional, however, you can go ahead and use the deprecated tags and tag attributes. You can always pick up CSS later if you decide to strengthen your Web authoring skills. For now, it's enough to master the basics of HTML as quickly and painlessly as possible.

HTML's growing distance from display controls is also evident in a shift away from **presentational elements** (also known as **physical elements**) in favor of the more abstract **informational elements**.

Presentational Elements

`<b></b>`

The `BOLDFACE` element darkens any text inside the tag-pair.

`<i></i>`

The `ITALICS` element italicizes any text inside the tag-pair.

Informational Elements

`<strong></strong>`

Most browsers treat the `STRONG` element as synonymous with the `BOLDFACE` element, but it can be rendered in different ways depending on the browser. For example, if a browser is making a text-to-voice conversion, the `STRONG` element might be rendered in a higher tone of voice.

`<em></em>`

Most browsers treat the `EMPHASIS` element as synonymous with the `ITALICS` element, but it can be rendered in different ways depending on the browser. For example, if a browser is making a text-to-voice conversion, the EMPHASIS element might be rendered in a louder tone of voice.

Any number of these text display elements and attributes can be combined by nesting multiple elements. For example, you can create boldface italics by nesting a pair of EMPHASIS tags inside a pair of STRONG tags (or vice-versa—it doesn't matter). Just be careful to unwind each nested tag-pair from the inside out when you insert the closing tags, thereby ensuring that the pairs are properly nested inside one another:

```
<em><strong>this is right</strong></em>
<em><strong>this is wrong</em></strong>
```

Table 2.2 lists selected type-related elements.

Table 2.2   Selected Type-Related Elements

HTML Element	Attributes	Attribute Values	What the Attribute Does
`<font></font>`	`face=`	[the name of a preinstalled type font]	Changes the typeface.
	`color=`	[a color name or hexadecimal color code]	Changes the text color.
	`size=`	n (an integer between 1 and 7) +n or −n	Changes the text size.
`<b></b>` (boldface)			
`<i></i>` (italics)			
`<strong></strong>`			
`<em></em>` (emphasis)			

◎◎ List Elements

Chapter titles and paragraphs are familiar tools for all writers, but Web page authors tend to use lists more frequently than other authors do—and with good reason. Lists of hyperlinks are a common fixture on many Web pages because they are so useful as a navigational device. For example, a large Web site might start with a list of links that operates as a "clickable" table of contents. Although you aren't ready to add any links to a Web page (Chapter Four covers hyperlinks), you can at least see how to format a table of contents for a Web site using HTML list elements.

Two types of lists commonly found on Web pages are the bulleted list (each list item is preceded by a bullet) and the enumerated list (each list item is numbered). Bulleted lists are created with the **unordered list element**, and enumerated lists are created with the **ordered list element**. You use the tags `<ul></ul>` to specify an unordered list and the tags `<ol></ol>` to establish an ordered list. Figure 2.4 shows how such lists differ from each other.

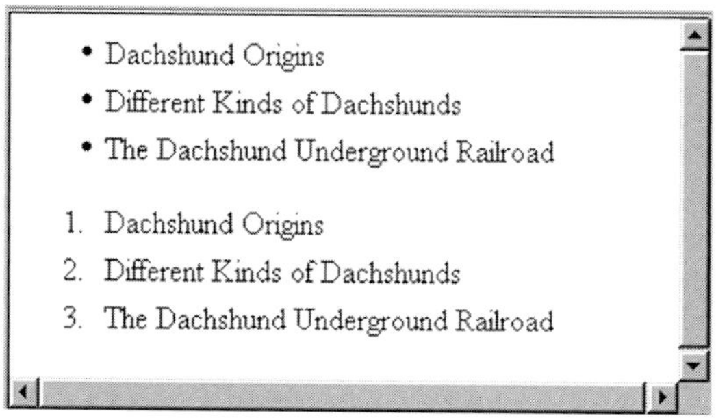

```
<ul>
   <li>Dachshund Origins</li>
   <li>Different Kinds of Dachshunds</li>
   <li>The Dachshund Underground Railroad</li>
</ul>
<ol>
   <li>Dachshund Origins</li>
   <li>Different Kinds of Dachshunds</li>
   <li>The Dachshund Underground Railroad</li>
</ol>
```

Figure 2.4 Two Types of Lists

Each **list-item element** inside the list must be marked with the list item tag-pair, `<li></li>`. Just as you can leave a paragraph tag-pair unclosed, so you can also leave the list item tag-pair open. However, XHTML requires `</li>`, so it may be a good idea to include these tags now—if only for the sake of any pages that may require a conversion later. Note that the list item elements are indented to set them off from any surrounding text.

Useful attributes are available for both ordered lists and unordered lists. You can label the list items in an ordered list with Arabic numerals, uppercase letters, lowercase letters, large Roman numerals, or small Roman numerals by setting the appropriate type attribute values inside the OL tag— 1, A, a, I, and i, respectively. (The default value is 1 for Arabic numerals.) You can also change the bullet shapes used in an unordered list by setting type attribute values inside the UL tag. Possible values are `disc`, `circle`, and `square`. (The default value is `disc`.) In addition, you can control the point at which an ordered list starts counting by set-

☆ WARNING Be Careful with Tag-Pairs

We've seen some examples of HTML tag-pairs that can be left unclosed without dire consequences (for example, `<p></p>` and `<li></li>`). Don't assume that this is the case for all HTML tag-pairs. In some cases, the HTML standard designates a closing tag as optional; in other cases, the closing tag is required. If you omit a closing tag for an element that requires it, some browsers may produce dramatically different and unpredictable results.

ting the `start` attribute in the OL tag. (See Figure 2.6 and Exercise 2 at the end of this chapter for examples of these list element attributes in action.)

A third type of list can be used for definitions or other list items that require longer descriptions. A **definition list element** is created with the tag-pair `<dl></dl>`. Inside the definition list, **deflist-term elements** are marked with the tag `<dt>`. In addition to the deflist-term elements, **deflist-definition elements** are marked with the tag `<dd>`. The deflist-definition introduces a definition (or perhaps a more general description) of its associated deflist-term. Deflist-term elements and deflist-definition elements work together in pairs inside the definition list.

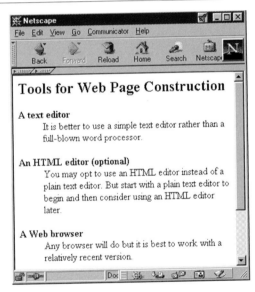

```
<h2>Tools for Web Page Construction</h2>
<dl>
   <dt><b>A text editor</b></dt>
      <dd> It is better to use a simple
text editor rather than a full-blown
word processor.<p>
      </dd>
   <dt><b>An HTML editor (optional)</b></dt>
      <dd>You may opt to use an HTML editor
```

Figure 2.5 A Definition List (*continues*)

```
instead of a plain text editor. But
start with a plain text editor to
begin and then consider using an HTML
editor later.<p>
    </dd>
 <dt><b>A Web browser</b></dt>
    <dd> Any browser will do but it is
best to work with a relatively recent
version.<p>
    </dd>
</dl>
```

Figure 2.5 A Definition List

In Figure 2.5, the deflist has been enhanced with boldface and paragraph elements that operate in conjunction with the deflist elements. Deflist-term elements are always left-justified and terminate with carriage returns. The deflist-definition elements are indented and terminate with a carriage return. These indentations set off the deflist-term definitions, making for easy reading. White space is a powerful visual device that can be used to great advantage on a Web page. We will describe additional HTML elements that manipulate white space shortly.

Nested list elements can be used for representing hierarchies. Each level of nesting introduces another level of indentation. By nesting ordered lists and differentiating them with the TYPE attribute, you can create a traditional document outline (see Figure 2.6). Table 2.3 describes some of HTML's list-related elements.

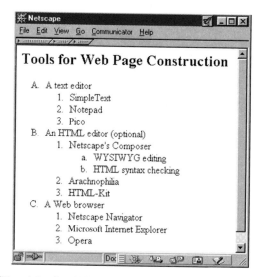

Figure 2.6 A Traditional Outline Using Nested Ordered Lists

Table 2.3   List-Related Elements

HTML Element	Attributes	Attribute Values	What the Attribute Does
`<ul></ul>` (unordered list)	`type=`	`disc`, `circle`, `square`	Changes the shape of the bullet. The default value is disc.
`<ol></ol>` (ordered list)	`type=`	`1`	Labels list items with Arabic numerals (the default type value).
		`A`	Labels list items with uppercase letters.
		`a`	Labels list items with lowercase letters.
		`I`	Labels list items with large Roman numerals.
		`i`	Labels list items with small Roman numerals.
	`start=`	`n` (a positive integer)	Indicates where to start counting.
`<li></li>` (list item)	`type=`	[any of the values associated with the type attribute for ordered lists]	Overrides any type attributes set by a relevant `OL` tag (applies only to ordered lists).
	`type=`	[any of the values associated with the type attribute for unordered lists]	Overrides any type attributes set by a relevant `UL` tag (applies only to unordered lists).
	`value=`	`n` (a positive integer)	Indicates where to start counting (applies only to ordered lists).
`<dl></dl>` (definition list)			
`<dt></dt>` (deflist-term)			
`<dd></dd>` (deflist-definition)			

◎◎ Controlling White Space

Sometimes what's not there is every bit as important as what is there. In the world of Web page construction, "what's not there" is called white space. Earlier in this chapter we saw how headings, paragraphs, and list elements take advantage of white space to facilitate text comprehension. Although these elements are useful for white-space management, they are limited to specific formatting patterns. Sometimes, however, a Web page author needs to fine-tune a text layout by inserting individual spaces and carriage returns.

Web browsers are programmed to ignore all extraneous spaces and blank lines in an `.html` file. For this reason, special HTML elements are needed to produce spaces and blank lines that will be preserved and displayed by a Web browser. These elements are, in fact, crucial for some Web page layouts.

To produce a single blank space, you can insert a special character that creates a **nonbreaking white space**. This special character, which is written ` ` (the ampersand and semi-colon are part of the name), is guaranteed to produce a single white space wherever it appears in an .html file. If you need three blank spaces in a row, for example, you would string three nonbreaking white-space characters together: `   `

☆**TIP**   **Special Characters**

The nonbreaking white-space character is just one of many special characters available to Web page authors. If you need an umlaut or an ampersand, consult a directory of special characters for HTML. Even if the desired character is available on your keyboard, you may still need a special character to make it visible on your Web page. For example, a pair of angle brackets `<like these>` will be treated as an HTML tag by all Web browsers unless you write them as follows: `&lt;like these&gt;`.

☆**TIP**   `<p><p><p><p><p>` = `<p>`

If you want to display a group of blank lines on your Web page, don't bother with multiple paragraph `<p>` tags. A string of `<p>` tags will produce only one blank line, no matter how many you use. To insert more than one blank line in your Web page display, use multiple `<br>` tags.

To terminate a line of text, and move to the following line, insert a **line break element**: `<br>`. If you need a blank line, insert two line breaks: `<br><br>`. If you need two blank lines in a row, insert three line breaks: `<br><br><br>`.

While indented lists stand out nicely, sometimes you may want to indent a single sentence or a paragraph of text that is not part of a list. The **block quote element** uses a `<blockquote></blockquote>` tag-pair to indent a text block. It is appropriate for setting off quotations, important instructions, or anything else to which you want to draw attention.

According to the HTML standard, the block quote element requires that the text inside the block quote be tagged by some other HTML element (for example, a paragraph tag-pair). In practice, most browsers will display a block quote even if you ignore this requirement. If you prefer, you can achieve the same text indentation with a single `<ul></ul>` tag-pair.

Finally, there may be times when you want the Web browser to re-create text with the spacing and line breaks preserved exactly as you originally typed them. For example, poetry and computer code require precise control over white space. Of course, you don't want to painstakingly insert a hundred nonbreaking white-space characters to do the job. In these situations, you can use the **preformat element** with the `<pre></pre>` tag-pair (see Figure 2.7).

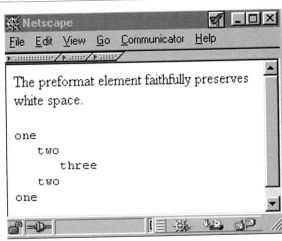

```
The preformat element faithfully preserves white space.
<pre>
one
   two
       three
   two
one
</pre>
```

Figure 2.7 The Preformat Element Preserves All Original White Space

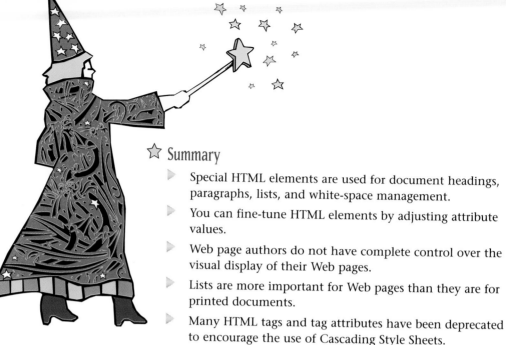

☆ Summary

▷ Special HTML elements are used for document headings, paragraphs, lists, and white-space management.

▷ You can fine-tune HTML elements by adjusting attribute values.

▷ Web page authors do not have complete control over the visual display of their Web pages.

▷ Lists are more important for Web pages than they are for printed documents.

▷ Many HTML tags and tag attributes have been deprecated to encourage the use of Cascading Style Sheets.

☆ Online References

Names for Colors (all safe for Internet Explorer and Navigator)
`http://users.rcn.com/giant.interport/COLOR/1ColorSpecifier.html`

A Reference Page for Special Characters
`http://www.ramsch.org/martin/uni/fmi-hp/iso8859-1.html`

CSS Quick Tutorial
`http://www.htmlhelp.com/reference/css/quick-tutorial.html`

Mulder's Stylesheets Tutorial
`http://hotwired.lycos.com/webmonkey/authoring/stylesheets/tutorials/tutorial1.html`

The Web Isn't for Everyone ... Yet
`http://hotwired.lycos.com/webmonkey/design/site_building/tutorials/tutorial5.html`

XHTML: What Exactly Is This Thing?
`http://htmlgoodies.earthweb.com/tutors/xhtml.html`

What Is XML?
`http://www.htmlgoodies.com/tutors/xml.html`

☆ Review Questions

1. Describe three ways that **HEADING** elements change the normal text display.

2. Which is larger, an `<h3>` heading or an `<h2>` heading?

3. Name four HTML elements that indent text. What tags or tag-pairs mark these elements?

4. What is the difference between the `<ol></ol>` tag-pair and the `<ul></ul>` tag-pair?

5. Which two HTML elements work together as a pair inside the definition list element?

6. Explain how to mark a block of text so that you can be sure everyone will see it in Geneva (the font—not the city).

7. Describe two ways to make a word (a) boldface, (b) italic, and (c) boldface italic.

8. How could you create a Web page display with five blank lines following a paragraph of text?

9. Explain the difference between a `<p>` tag and a `<br>` tag.

10. Which HTML element is the best choice for displaying a poem when line breaks and indentations are an important part of the poem?

☆ Hands-On Exercises

1. Use paragraph elements to construct a Web page that looks like this:

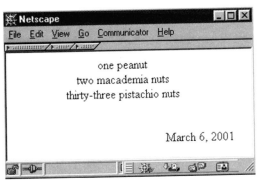

2. Use list elements and font elements to construct a Web page that looks like this:

3. Use nested list elements with the type attribute to construct a Web page that produces the display shown in Figure 2.6.

4. Consult a list of special characters for HTML and find the special characters for the following:

   (a) An ampersand (&)
   (b) A percent sign (%)
   (c) A tilde (~)
   (d) An asterisk (*)
   (e) An equals sign (=)

   Next, create a Web page that displays the following line:

   50% of 32 = 4**2 && ~T = F

5. Construct a Web page that looks like this:

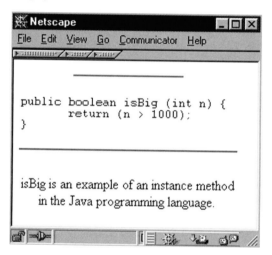

CHAPTER THREE

COLORS, PATTERNS, AND INLINE GRAPHICS

A Web page without graphics can contain valuable information and useful hyperlinks, but black type on a white background is as disappointing as a gray sparrow in a tropical rain forest. Happily, no one has to be an artist to dress up a Web page. Adding a colored background and an image or two can make a dramatic difference for your audience. Such enhancements are not difficult to achieve, and they will make your Web pages look like they belong on the Web.

Chapter Objectives

☆ Demonstrate how to add colors to a Web page

☆ Explain how to add background patterns

☆ Show how to add images to a Web Page

☆ Explain the use of relative addresses for image files

☆ Investigate the interplay between design decisions and bandwidth consumption

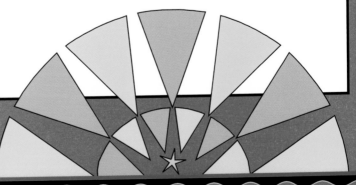

◎◎ Colors and Color Codes

The easiest way to dress up a page of text is by adding a background color or pattern. When you tell a Web browser to color the background of a Web page, you have a choice of 16,777,216 colors. If that variety seems overwhelming, you can select one of the 216 "Web-safe" colors—that is, colors that can be faithfully reproduced on any computer monitor regardless of the operating systems. You can also apply a pattern to the background of your Web page, and here the choices are limitless. It takes only a second to set a background color or a background pattern for a Web page, yet these features can bring a vibrant personality to your site.

Hexadecimal and RGB Color Codes

All Web browsers use the same coding system for describing colors. The code is based on **hexadecimal notation**, which represents integers in a base 16 notation (instead of the usual base 10, or decimal, notation). Each color code contains six digits, where each digit is one of 16 possible alphanumeric characters (0123456789ABCDEF). With six digits and 16 possible digit values, we can describe 16,777,216 ($16 \times 16 \times 16 \times 16 \times 16 \times 16$) different colors. To match a code to a particular color, you can visit any number of Web sites that display color wheels or color charts (see the URL list at the end of this chapter).

☆**WARNING** **Color Charts in Books**

The color charts with hexadecimal codes found in books are convenient, but it is difficult to reproduce colors on paper and have them exactly match their appearance on your display monitor. Colors on paper are good approximations, but when you view a color chart on your computer monitor, you'll see the colors exactly as they'll appear on your Web page.

If you want to add a background color to a Web page, include a **BGCOLOR** attribute in the BODY element, with a code string for the attribute value (see Figure 3.1):

Note that each hexadecimal code is preceded by a pound (#) character and is enclosed in double quotes. The # lets browsers know that they are about to read a hexadecimal code, and it is required by HTML.

Hexadecimal codes may look odd, but the color codes are actually quite simple. Each six-digit code string stands for a series of three integers, with two hexadecimal digits representing each integer. For example, the code "DA4900" represents the integers DA, 49, and 0 ("0" is written "00" to ensure that we always use two digits—whether we need them or not). You can easily convert these hexadecimal integers to decimal integers if you are familiar with base 16 notation (to convert "DA4900" you need to know that "D" represents 13 and "A" represents 10 in base 16) :

DA = 13 (16) + 10 (1) = 208 + 10 = 218

49 = 4 (16) + 9 (1) = 64 + 9 = 73

00 = 0 (16) + 0 (1) = 0 + 0 = 0

`<body bgcolor="#FFFF88">` creates a Web page with a pale yellow background.

`<body bgcolor="#000088">` creates a Web page with a dark blue background.

`<body bgcolor="#66AA94">` creates a Web page with a gray-blue background.

`<body bgcolor="#01F694">` creates a Web page with a light green background.

`<body bgcolor="#DA4900">` creates a Web page with an orange-brown background.

`<body bgcolor="#AA33CC">` creates a Web page with a lavender background.

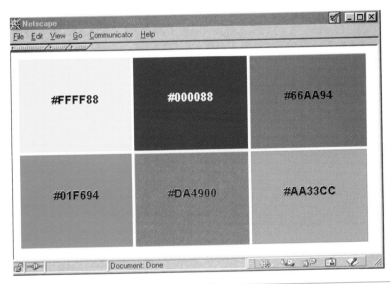

Figure 3.1 Some Hexadecimal Color Codes

☆**TIP**   **Default Background Colors**

It is a good idea to explicitly assign a background color to all of your Web pages. Different browsers can assign different background colors to pages where the background color has not been specified. Although white is typically the default, older versions of Netscape Navigator used a gray background. Because you can't know which browser will be used to view your Web pages, you should control the background color by including an explicit background attribute on all of your Web pages.

We could then rewrite the hexadecimal triple (DA, 49, 00) as a decimal triple (218, 73, 0). Some graphics software packages work with decimal triples instead of hexadecimal codes. The decimal codes are called **RGB (red-green-blue) notation**. Hexadecimal codes and RGB codes are equivalent notational systems—that is, any color described by one notation can be described by the other notation. Not all color systems are equivalent, however. For example, the familiar system of primary colors is based on **RYB** (**Red-Yellow-Blue**) notation, which is not the same as RGB. (The list of URLs at the end of this chapter gives the source of an article that explains how RGB and RYB differ from each other.)

☆ **TIP**   **24-Bit Color**

Software and hardware documentation sometimes mentions "24-bit color" displays. In such systems, the full spectrum of all hexadecimal color codes can be displayed. With base 2 integers (which are equivalent to binary or "bit" strings), it takes four binary digits to represent the numbers 0 to 15. Since 0–15 is also the range of integers that can be represented by one hexadecimal digit, it follows that 24 bits are needed to represent six hexadecimal digits (4 bits per digit × 6 digits = 24 bits). Although preference settings for file options or monitor displays may refer to "millions of colors," that's just a user-friendly way of saying "24-bit color."

Web-Safe Colors

All browsers are programmed to display all of the legal hexadecimal color codes, but wise Web designers understand that some colors are safer than others. *Safe colors* are colors that are displayed consistently by any operating system. Not all colors can be counted on to look the same on different software platforms and hardware configurations. In fact, the differences may sometimes be dramatic. For example, a color code that produces a reddish-brown on a laptop running Windows 95 may look like dull brown without any red at all on a Macintosh desktop. These differences do not always matter. If you are working with a trademark or a logo, however, dramatic color variations may be much less tolerable.

Web designers generally prefer to work with a set of 216 **Web-safe colors** that are displayed consistently on all types of computers. Computer monitors are generally inconsistent in terms of their color palettes. Although two monitors may each support a palette of 16,777,216 colors (sometimes called "true color"), they won't necessarily display the exact same set of 16,777,216 colors.

All modern color monitors support eight-bit color (256 colors). So why are there 216 Web-safe colors instead of 256? Computer hardware makes it convenient to work with powers of 2 (for example, $2^8 = 256$) but software designers need to work with color cubes. A *color cube* is a symbol system for colors characterized by discrete values in three independent dimensions (because RGB representations are based on three dimensions). Each dimension must support the same number of values, so color cubes must be designed to represent a fixed number of colors where that fixed number is a cube (for example, $2^3 = 8$, $3^3 = 27$). As luck would have it, the largest cube that does not exceed 256 is $6^3 = 216$. That's why we have 216 Web-safe colors.

☆ **WARNING**   **Windows and Macintosh Computers**

Although Web-safe colors are relatively consistent, even these colors are not perfectly consistent across all computers. Variations can arise even with the Web-safe colors. For example, Windows users tend to see colors with more intense hues and Macintosh users generally see colors that are more subdued. Professional Web designers must sometimes grapple with these differences, but the rest of us generally need understand only that Web-Safe colors are at least safer than arbitrary colors. To learn more about the dark side of Web-safe colors, consult the URLs at the end of this chapter.

It's easy to recognize a Web-safe color in its hexadecimal notation. Each Web-safe color is based on component integers that span the maximal spectrum from 00 to FF (0–255 in base 10). When you divide this numerical range into six equidistant values, the resulting values are 00, 33, 66, 99, CC, and FF. Web-safe colors, then, consist of all the hexadecimal codes made up of three double-digits, excluding all digits that are not divisible by 3 (that is, 99CC33 or 00FF66 are Web-safe, but 880033 and 33CC93 are not).

Recall from Chapter Two that you can specify some colors by name when changing text colors. Those same color names can serve as background attribute values as well. Figure 3.2 shows the most commonly used color names with their respective colors.

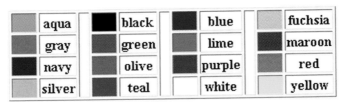

Figure 3.2 Color Names for BGCOLOR Attribute Values

Adding Background Patterns

Adding a background *pattern* is as easy as adding a background color, except that you use a **BACKGROUND** attribute inside the **BODY** tag, and you must specify a graphics file that holds the desired background pattern. You can find free background files on the Web, or you can make your own with graphics software such as Microsoft Paint or from digital images captured with a camera.

You may be surprised to find that photographs of mundane objects can be the basis for interesting background patterns. Browsers display backgrounds by filling the available space in the browser's window with a tiling of the background image. A **tiling** is a pattern created by repeating the same image to fill up a particular space. When the tiled image has small dimensions, the tiling pattern may be obvious because of visible repetition and possible boundary effects. When the tiled image has large dimensions, you can fill up a small browser window without any repetition.

☆**TIP**   **Tiling Images Should Download Quickly**

The background for a Web page should display as quickly as possible, which can happen if the image downloads rapidly. Keep your background files as small as possible with respect to memory (and bandwidth) requirements. Images with smaller dimensions generally consume much less memory than images with larger dimensions, but the bottom line is how much memory the image requires. As a rule, avoid background images that are larger than 10KB, and whenever possible, try to keep your background files smaller than 5KB.

If you pick an image that contains obvious contours and shapes, repetition and image boundaries will make the tiling apparent. In addition, images based on photographs often produce a "pillow" effect when the colors along opposite edges don't match up well. Figure 3.3 shows a tiling based on an image that is 298 pixels wide and 196 pixels high. This image is an unretouched photograph of an oil spill on a wet road. Although the image is interesting, the obvious boundaries in its tiling are not desirable.

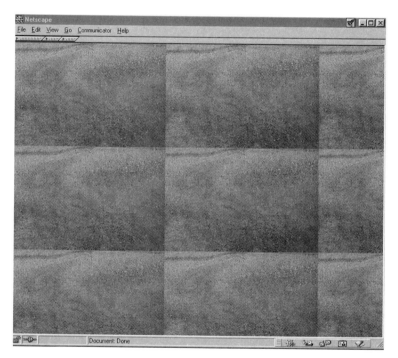

Figure 3.3 All Backgrounds Are Based on Tiled Images

If you want to use photographs for your background tilings, look for images that are relatively uniform in color, especially along their edges. Even then, the tiling effect may be apparent in pattern repetitions. Figure 3.4 shows a background based on a photograph of water in a swimming pool. Although this tiling has a clear pattern, the boundaries around each tile are much less apparent here than in Figure 3.3.

If the tiling pattern is small and uniform, tiling repetitions will not be overly obvious. For this reason, wallpaper patterns are often fine-grained to avoid distracting repetition. One way to restrict yourself to appropriate images is to select images primarily for their texture. For example, consider Figure 3.5, which shows an example based on a photograph of an old barn wall.

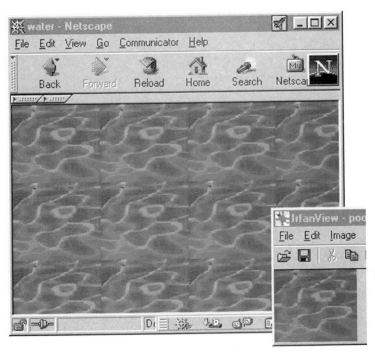

Figure 3.4 Uniform Colors Reduce the Tiling Effect

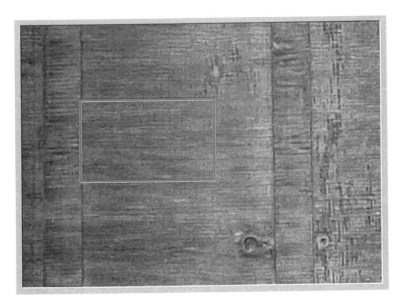

Figure 3.5 Cropping a Small Area from a Photograph

Using a graphics utility, crop an area from the image that looks reasonably uniform in color and patterning. Remember—any irregularities in the image will give rise to discernable patterns. Even though the region marked in Figure 3.5 looks quite uniform, when it is tiled on a Web page, you can readily see vertical boundaries marking the joint between the left and right edges of the image (see Figure 3.6). On the other hand, the top and bottom edges of the tiled image mesh very naturally and show no horizontal boundaries.

☆ **TIP**   **Use Both a Background Color and a Background Image**

Even the smallest background file will require some downloading time over a slow Internet connection. One way to make your page look good during the wait is to set up a BGCOLOR attribute in addition to the BACKGROUND attribute. The background color will display immediately, dressing up the page display while the background image is still downloading. When the background pattern is eventually ready to display, it will replace the background color.

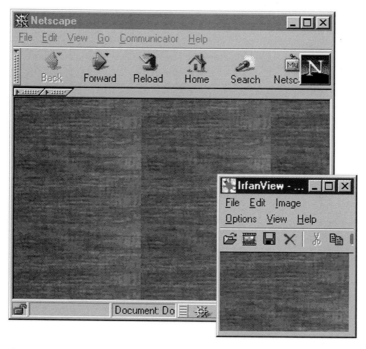

Figure 3.6 Tiling Boundaries Are Usually Undesirable in a Background Display

You can often minimize such boundary effects in tiling patterns by using an image editor (such as Adobe Photoshop or Softkey PhotoFinish). Using a color picker tool (also known as an eyedropper), sample a color on one of the boundary edges (for example, on the right edge of the image). Next, use a paintbrush or pencil tool to add some of that color to the corresponding region on the opposite edge (for example, on the left edge of the image). By blending the two regions surrounding the boundary edges, you can eliminate visible boundaries in the tiled pattern. Figure 3.7 shows an edited version of the file shown in Figure 3.6, after the boundary effect has been removed. A hue adjustment was also made to add some color.

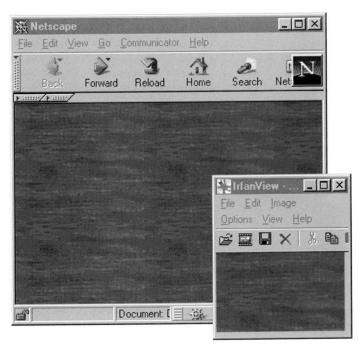

Figure 3.7 An Image Editor Can Be Used to Remove Boundary Effects

Some photographs produce seamless or near-seamless tiling patterns without any editing. Such images tend to be consistent in coloration, but have patterns that do not require precise matchups at the boundaries. The background in Figure 3.8 was created with an unretouched photograph of some vegetation. Can you detect the tile boundaries?

If you add text to a Web page with a background, be careful to ensure that the text is legible against the background. Use contrasting colors for text and an adequate font size. Large background patterns require very large text fonts (see Figure 3.8). Even quiet backgrounds, however, may drown out too-small text. Use simple sans serif fonts and avoid busy page layouts on top of busy background patterns.

One good way to make a memorable statement with a background is to run a pattern down the left side of a Web page while using a solid color as the background for the rest of the page. If you pick an image file that is wide enough, a tiling of that image will repeat the image only along the vertical dimension, and the pattern will appear only on the left side of the page. The Web page shown in Figure 3.9 uses a background image that is 18 pixels high and 999 pixels wide. We will return to this use of background files in Chapter Six when we consider the use of tables to control the positioning of text on a Web page.

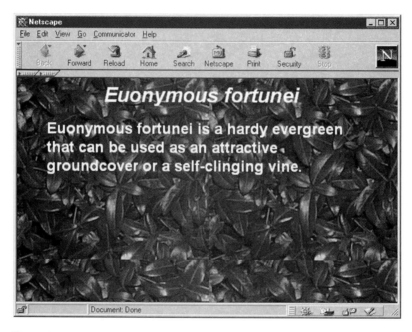

Figure 3.8 Some Tilings Don't Exhibit Obvious Boundary Effects

☆**TIP**   **Backgrounds Should Take a Back Seat to Foregrounds**

Sometimes a background looks great by itself but commands too much attention on the completed Web page. For most Web pages, the ideal background is noticeable, but just barely. It should never dominate the page, interfere with the readability of text, or distract visitors from more important page elements. As a rule, pale, washed-out backgrounds are preferred; dark backgrounds tend to dominate a page. Backgrounds that are too busy are another bad idea. When in doubt, tone it down.

In Chapter Six, we will also see how to embed text inside tables for maximal readability on top of background patterns. The backgrounds in Figures 3.4 and 3.8 are too intense for direct text overlays, unless the text in question is very large and bold. Adding tables to your layout makes it possible to combine small text with vibrant backgrounds without sacrificing the readability of the text.

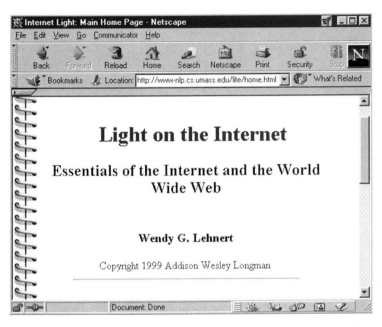

Figure 3.9 A Very Wide Background Image Produces a Border for a Web Page

◎◎ Inline Images

Images for the Web can be obtained with digital cameras, from image libraries on the Web (see the list of URLs at the end of this chapter), by digitizing a photograph or drawing with a scanner, or by creating your own computer art with a drawing program like Microsoft Paint. When creating your own image files for the Web, you should choose a Web-friendly file format. You may use GIF, JPEG (JPG), or PNG files for Web page images. You cannot use BMP, TIFF, or PICT files. In addition, you should try to work with images that are no larger than 30–40KB whenever possible. Chapter Five discusses file formats for images and tools for reducing their bandwidth requirements in more depth. For now, we will concentrate on the HTML that allows you to insert an image on a Web page and control its appearance on that page.

The IMG element is used to place images on Web pages. A SRC (source) attribute inside the IMG tag specifies the name of the file that contains the image. For

☆WARNING **Don't Break the Law**

Although it is easy to copy image files from other people's Web pages, you cannot legally add those images to your own Web pages without obtaining the owner's permission. If you publish an unauthorized image on the Web, you may be breaking the law by violating a copyright protection.

example, suppose you have an image file named `donut.gif`. You can add it to a Web page with the tag `<img src="donut.gif">`. Image tags belong in the Web page `BODY`, and the placement of the tag within the `BODY` determines its positioning on the Web page. To understand how browsers place images on Web pages, you must first understand how images are represented as elements in an `HTML` file.

An **inline image** is an image that is treated as a single, alphanumeric character, just like a character created when you press keys on a keyboard. Each `IMG` element creates an inline image on your Web page. If you place an `IMG` tag between two sentences, the image associated with that tag will be inserted between those sentences as if it were just another typed character. The major difference between the inline image and the characters surrounding it is its size. An inserted image is typically much larger than the characters in your Web page display, which forces the Web browser to rework the placement of text around the image. Figure 3.10 shows what happens when an inline image is positioned in the middle of a paragraph.

```
The dachshund was originally used to hunt
badgers, wild boar, foxes, and rabbits.
<img src="donut.gif"
  alt="a dachshund profile">
```

> The `IMG` element is used to insert inline images into a Web page.

```
The name "dachshund" means "badger dog" in German, where
these dogs were first bred. Woodcuts and paintings from
the fifteenth century show badgers being hunted by dogs
with short legs, long bodies, and hound-like ears.
```

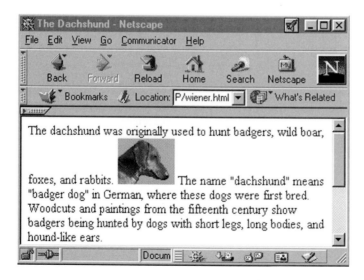

Figure 3.10 An Inline Graphic

> **☆WARNING   Where's My Image?**
>
> Sometimes a Web page will display a box with a broken image icon (a red X or question mark) where your image is supposed to appear, but no image. If your SRC attribute specifies a filename like that in Figure 3.10, verify that the file is located in the same subdirectory as your HTML file. If both files do not reside in the same subdirectory, your browser will not be able to find your image (but see the end of this chapter for more about referencing image files inside SRC attributes).

The Web browser needs to make room for this oversized inline graphic, so it increases the vertical space set aside for the text line that contains the graphic. This display is a reasonable rendering of the HTML file, given no additional directives, but it is probably not the best way to combine text and graphics.

> **☆TIP   Some Browsers Don't Display Graphics**
>
> Whenever you add an image to a Web page, you should always include a short text description of each image inside the IMG tag. The **ALT attribute** (see Figure 3.10) allows you to specify a line of text that will be displayed by browsers that aren't configured to display graphics. For example, browsers designed for visually impaired users rely on text-to-voice speech generation to describe Web pages. Text-to-voice browsers resort to the ALT attribute whenever they encounter an image. The ALT attribute will also be displayed in place of your image if a problem with your image file arises.

Aligning Images

Inline images need to be aligned within text blocks to achieve a pleasing combination of text and graphics. This effect is produced by placing the ALIGN attribute inside the IMG tag (see Figure 3.11). When you include an ALIGN attribute in the <img> tag, any text near that image will automatically flow around the image—generally, the preferred display. You can also control the vertical alignment of an image relative to its text baseline by using the ALIGN values BOTTOM, TOP, and MIDDLE.

You can exert additional control over text behavior around an image by inserting a CLEAR attribute inside the BR tag. When it encounters a BR tag with CLEAR=LEFT, the browser immediately interrupts the flow of text and resumes it on the next available line that has no image set against the left margin. With the use of CLEAR=RIGHT, text is resumed on the next available line that has no image set against the right margin. To drop the text to the next available line with no images on either margin, use CLEAR=CENTER.

```
<img src="donut.gif" alt="a dachshund profile"
 width="70" height="54"
 align="left" >
```

> `align="left"` allows text to flow down around the right side of a left-justified inline image.

The dachshund was originally used to hunt badgers, wild boar, foxes, and rabbits.

```
<img src="woodcut2.gif" alt="an old woodcut of a hunt"
 width="219" height="232"
 align="right" >
```

> `align="right"` allows text to flow down around the left side of a right-justified inline image.

The name "dachshund" means "badger dog" in German, where these dogs were first bred. Woodcuts and paintings from the fifteenth century show badgers being hunted by dogs with short legs, long bodies, and hound-like ears. To this day, the dachshund's short muscular legs are well suited for burrowing into tunnels and underground lairs, although the breed has never been active as a hunting dog in the United States. As pets, dachshunds are lively, loyal, and assertive watchdogs.

Figure 3.11 Use the ALIGN Attribute to Make Text Flow around Images

Scaling Images

Sometimes, an image may not be the right size for your Web page. It might be too big or perhaps not big enough. In such cases, you need to **scale** the image—that is, resize it by increasing or decreasing its dimensions on the Web page. You can easily adjust the amount of space allocated for an image by changing its WIDTH and HEIGHT attributes. To produce a larger image, increase the attributes' values. To create a smaller image, decrease them. The woodcut image shown in Figure 3.11 was scaled from its original dimensions, 876 × 927 pixels, to a smaller size, 219 × 232 pixels, by dividing the original height and width by 4.

> ☆ **TIP**   **Always Include WIDTH and HEIGHT Attributes**
>
> Even if you don't need to scale an image to change its display size, you should always specify the image's width and height inside the IMG tag. We will explain why in a few pages, when we examine page layouts and incremental displays.

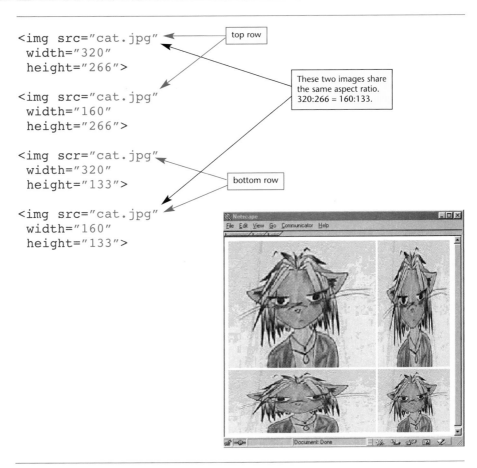

Figure 3.12 gives the following code with annotations:

```
<img src="cat.jpg"          ← top row
  width="320"
  height="266">

<img src="cat.jpg"
  width="160"
  height="266">

<img scr="cat.jpg"
  width="320"
  height="133">          ← bottom row

<img src="cat.jpg"
  width="160"
  height="133">
```

These two images share the same aspect ratio. 320:266 = 160:133.

Figure 3.12 Incorrect Scaling Results in Distorted Images

When you resize an image, you must be careful to preserve the **aspect ratio** (the height-to-width ratio) so that the resized image does not become distorted. Figure 3.12 shows an image that has been scaled twice correctly and twice incorrectly (that is, without preserving the original aspect ratio). You can generally scale images down without an unacceptable loss of image quality, although extreme downsizing will eventually result in a hard-to-see image. If you go in the opposite direction, inflating an image by scaling its dimensions upward, you may begin to see a "pixelation effect," in which large, uniform blocks of color replace finer details. If this effect occurs, you have enlarged the image beyond its resolution level—there just isn't enough information in the image to fill up the space. As a rule, high-resolution images can be enlarged to a greater degree than low-resolution images.

Finally, note that shrinking an image by scaling it down *does not* reduce its bandwidth requirements. To reduce download times, you must *compress* the image, as discussed in Chapter 5.

Table 3.1 summarizes the HTML elements related to colors, patterns, and images.

☆ **SHORTCUT**   **Finding an Image's Dimensions**

If you have an image file but aren't sure of its dimensions, open it up using your Web browser. You may see the width and height in the title bar of the browser window, or you can find out this information by selecting Page Info on the View menu. Let your browser tell you what you need to know.

Table 3.1   Selected Color, Pattern, and Image Elements

HTML Element	Attributes	Attribute Values	What the Attribute Does
`<body></body>`	`background=`	[a filename]	Sets the background pattern for the page.
	`bgcolor=`	[a color name or hexadecimal color code]	Sets the background color for the page.
`<img>`	`align=`	`left`, `right`	Alignment is used to justify the image against one side of the page with text flowing down alongside it.
	`alt=`	[a string of text]	The `alt` string is used by browsers that cannot display the image.
	`height=`	`n` (an integer)	Sets the height of the image in pixels.
	`src=`	[a filename]	Tells the browser which image file to display.
	`width=`	`n` (an integer)	Sets the width of the image in pixels.

Relative Paths and Image Files

When you add images to your Web pages, you necessarily add image files to your collection of HTML files. If your Web site is small, it makes sense to keep all of your files in the same directory. As the size of your Web site increases, however, it may make sense to organize your files using multiple file directories. In that case, you may need to make some adjustments to your IMG SRC attributes.

The value of an IMG element's SRC attribute tells a Web browser where it can find the image file that should be displayed. This location is always relative to the current URL being displayed (that is, the URL of the HTML file containing the IMG element).

```
<img src="donut.gif"
  alt="a dachshund profile"
  width="70" height="54"
```

> donut.gif must be in the same directory as the HTML file containing this tag.

If you want to insert an image file from a different directory, you can specify a relative path to the file's location, which browsers can then use to track down the file. Relative paths are always interpreted in the context of the current URL. If you add more directory names to the relative path location, those directories will be inserted into the current URL. Alternatively, you can instruct the browser to remove any number of directories from the current URL. Let's illustrate these possibilities with some examples.

First, we need to consider the baseline URL for the Web page displaying the image. All relative paths in the SRC attribute must be understood in the context of the baseline URL.

Consider the following baseline URL:

> The is the directory path portion of the baseline URL.

```
http://www.webland.com/workshops/wk3/ch8/ex4/summary.html
```

When we specify the SRC attribute as

> This relative path is identical to the baseline path.

```
src="donut.gif"
```

the browser looks for the file with the following path name:

```
http://www.webland.com/workshops/wk3/ch8/ex4/donut.gif
```

Next, suppose we specify a SRC attribute within a subdirectory. Using the same baseline URL, `http://www.webland.com/workshops/wk3/ch8/ex4/summary.html`

when we specify the SRC attribute as

`src="images/donut.gif"` ——————

> This relative path is longer than the baseline path.

the browser looks for the file with the following path name:

`http://www.webland.com/workshops/wk3/ch8/ex4/images/`
`donut.gif`

Alternatively, we can shorten the URL for the image file by using a "double-dot" notation. Let's work from the same baseline URL again:

`http://www.webland.com/workshops/wk3/ch8/ex4/summary.html`

When we specify the SRC attribute as

`src="../donut.gif"` ——————

> This relative path is shorter than the baseline path.

the browser looks for the file with the following path name:

`http://www.webland.com/workshops/wk3/ch8/donut.gif`

You can also remove multiple directories by including one set of double-dots for each directory to be eliminated:

`http://www.webland.com/workshops/wk3/ch8/ex4/summary.html`

If we remove three subdirectories,

`src="../../../donut.gif"` ——————

> This relative path is much shorter than the baseline path.

the browser will look for the file with the following path name:

`http://www.webland.com/workshops/donut.gif`

Next, we will combine double-dots with new directory names. In this case, we remove directories from the baseline first according to the number of double-dots used, and then we insert the directory names into the new URL.

`http://www.webland.com/workshops/wk3/ch8/ex4/summary.html`

We remove two, then add two subdirectories:

`src="../../ch13/ex9/donut.gif"` ——————

> This relative path is very different from the baseline path.

Now the browser will look for the file with the following path name:

`http://www.webland.com/workshops/wk3/cs13/ex9/donut.gif`

To store files for your Web site in multiple directories, you must duplicate the file structure used on your local computer (where you do your Web page development) on the Web server (where your pages will be made public). A relative link on your local host will not work on a Web server unless the same directory paths are also valid on the Web server.

◎◎ Coping with Bandwidth Limitations

If you are working on a high-bandwidth Internet connection, it is important to remember how different life is for users with 56K modems. More than 95% of all home computer users connect to the Internet via telephone modems. If a Web page contains only text, it will download quickly for everyone (the Web page can include approximately 30 single-spaced pages before its downloading time is likely to make anyone impatient). Web pages with images are another story, however.

In this section, we focus on some techniques that don't actually reduce download times, but rather minimize the amount of time your readers spend waiting for file downloads. In general, you want to keep your visitors occupied while file downloads are taking place. A 200KB image file can prove quite annoying if you have nothing to do while waiting for it to appear on your screen. Of course, the same transfer time won't matter if you are busy doing something else while the download takes place in the background.

Page Layouts and Incremental Displays

A Web browser tries to display as much information as it can as fast as it can. It doesn't have to wait until all of the elements of a Web page have been downloaded before it shows anything on-screen. Rather, a browser displays pages incrementally, showing whatever elements it can as soon as possible, based on whatever it knows about the final layout of the Web page. Web page authors can facilitate incremental page displays by ensuring that the browser receives essential page layout details long before all Web page elements have been downloaded.

An image can slow down a page display if the Web page author has not been careful to include its dimensions in the HTML code. If the dimensions of an image display are not explicitly available inside an IMG tag, the browser must wait until the image file has finished downloading before it can determine the image's dimensions and place it on the Web page. Moreover, the space requirements of the image must be known before any subsequent elements of the layout can be displayed. Thus not knowing the dimensions of a Web page image slows down the display of everything on the page that follows the image.

In contrast, if the browser knows the dimensions of all images on a page, it can work out the page layout and print the text for that page without having to wait for the image downloads. You can easily specify the dimensions of an image by using two IMG attributes: WIDTH and HEIGHT. The same attributes are used for image scaling (as described earlier). If your page contains both images and text, your Web site visitors can keep busy by perusing the text while the images download. People don't mind a few delayed image displays when they are happily engaged elsewhere.

Strategic Image Placement

Many novice Web page designers like to position a large, impressive image right at the top of a Web page. This inclination is certainly understandable: attention-grabbing images work well in magazines and newspapers. Unfortunately, a large image on a Web page will not appear immediately, especially for users who are downloading the page over a telephone line. It is never a good idea to present your audience with an empty Web page display and nothing to do while the page downloads. Thus the worst place to include a large image is at the very top of a Web page.

Always position large images somewhere other than the top of your Web page, unless perhaps you intend to employ one of the techniques described below. Even with these options, however, this placement remains a questionable design decision. Remember that your general goal is to keep your readers engaged and occupied at all times—especially during file downloads.

Interlaced GIFs and Progressive JPEGs

One way to make slow downloads less annoying is to use GIF and JPEG files that are displayed in increments while they are being downloaded. An **interlaced GIF** file produces its displays in four passes. The first pass produces a fuzzy version of the image. The next pass looks a bit better, and the final two passes present the complete file in full detail. This effect is typically achieved by displaying every tenth line of pixels on the first pass, every fifth line on the second pass, every other line on the third pass, and the complete image on the fourth pass. Progressive JPEGs operate in a similar fashion.

Incremental graphic displays can be interesting to watch and will pacify all but the most harried Web users. Many file utilities and GIF converters support an interlaced GIF option or progressive JPEG option. Look for a check box when you save the image to a file.

1 × 1 Pixel Images

Professional designers sometimes use a little trick to keep a steady flow of image files downloading in the background. This approach works when you have a Web site involving multiple Web pages, and you can anticipate the user taking a certain path or paths through the site. Normally, a user must download a Web page before the downloading of the images on that page will commence. You can, however, "trick" a browser into downloading image files for Web pages that haven't been requested yet by hiding invisible versions of those image files on Web pages viewed earlier.

Suppose you have a two-page Web site, with one page acting as a "front door" to your site. Moreover, suppose that visitors use a hyperlink on the first page to reach your second page. If the second page contains a large image file, you can scale this graphic down to a 1×1 pixel image, then insert that very tiny version of the image somewhere on your first Web page. It doesn't matter where this version appears, because an image that occupies only one pixel will not be visible to viewers of the Web page. By inserting a one-pixel version of your image on the first Web page, you ensure that browsers can start downloading the image while users are still viewing the first Web page. When those same users later click on the link for the second Web page, the image for the second Web page will (ideally) have finished downloading and be ready to display.

If you are very confident about the paths that users will follow through your site, you can anticipate page downloads and preload images by taking advantage of strategically placed 1×1 pixel images. Of course, you should still observe the warnings about placing large images at the top of Web pages—people may click through your site's pages faster on return visits than they did on their first visit. Try to anticipate all sorts of user pathing behavior when you employ this trick. Although you can't completely control the way in which visitors move through your site, you might be able to make your site less pokey for at least some percentage of your users.

☆ **WARNING Use 1 × 1 Pixel Images with Restraint**

If you overdo things by including too many 1×1 pixel images, the background downloads will slow down your visitors and make your site inexplicably pokey for people who don't benefit from your second-guessing. Although this technique can be useful, you should use it sparingly—and only in situations where you are very sure about the navigation patterns for your site.

☆ Summary

▷ Hexadecimal and RGB color codes are two different notations for the same coding system.

▷ Web-safe colors are displayed more consistently on various types of computers than are other colors.

▷ You can add background patterns to Web pages by tiling a single image across the page, but you should be aware that some images work better than others as background patterns.

▷ ALIGN, ALT, WIDTH, and HEIGHT are important attributes for the IMG element.

▷ File downloads need not bore your visitors if you plan your pages with an eye toward bandwidth consumption.

☆ Online References

Color Charts
http://www.hypersolutions.org/rgb.html

A Tutorial on Hexadecimal Notation
http://hotwired.lycos.com/webmonkey/97/17/index2a.html

RGB versus RYB
http://home.pacbell.net/dbldgt/electronics/theory/light/
rgbryb001.html

Names for Colors (Recognized by Internet Explorer and Navigator)
http://users.rcn.com/giant.interport/COLOR/
1ColorSpecifier.html

Death of the Web-Safe Color Palette?
http://hotwired.lycos.com/webmonkey/00/37/
index2a.html?tw=design

Dazzling Graphics for the Web
http://palfrey.userworld.com/dazzle/outline.html

Images for Web Pages
http://www.stars.com/Graphics/Images/

Graphics Software
http://www.cs.ubc.ca/spider/ladic/software.html

FreeFoto.com
http://www.freefoto.com/

☆ Review Questions

1. Which two notational systems are used to represent colors? Which one is used by Web browsers?

2. Which of the following are Web-safe colors?

   (a) 4400CC
   (b) 101010
   (c) FFFFFF
   (d) AABBCC
   (e) 500000

3. Which BODY attribute is used to set a background color for a Web page? Which BODY attribute is used to set a background pattern for a Web page?

4. Explain how browsers handle inline graphics when no formatting attributes are present. How can you control the placement of an image on a Web page?

5. Which IMG attribute makes text flow around an image? Which values can be assigned to that attribute?

6. Why is it important to include an ALT attribute in every IMG tag?

7. How do you scale an image? Can you reduce the bandwidth requirements for an image by scaling it down?

8. Suppose a Web page has the URL `http://www.usone.edu/ch10/exer.html` and an IMG tag on that page contains the attribute pair `SRC="../images/computer/pc12.gif"`. What is the full URL for the image file referenced by that IMG element?

9. How can you make a browser preload images for a Web page other than the current Web page?

10. What is an incremental Web page layout? How can a Web page author make sure that browsers will display a Web page incrementally?

☆ Hands-On Exercises

1. Visit `http://www.hypersolutions.org/rgb.html` and use the color code converter found at that site to find the hexadecimal equivalent for the following RGB code: 23, 200, 159. Then convert the hexadecimal code C70B48 into an RGB code. (*Note*: If you understand base 16 integers, you can do these conversions by hand.)

2. A 24-bit color display is capable of showing 256 times as many colors as a 16-bit color display. What is the difference between 24-bit color and 32-bit color? Visit `http://palfrey.userworld.com/dazzle/glossary.html` to find out whether your answer is correct.

3. If you design a Web page on a 17-inch monitor, your resulting Web pages may not look very good when viewed on a 14-inch monitor. Visit

`http://palfrey.userworld.com/dazzle/all.html#`
`Resolution` to find out how variations in screen resolution could affect
your choice of Web page images. What is the typical resolution setting for a
17-inch monitor? What is the typical resolution setting for a 14-inch monitor? If a certain image should never take up more than one-third of the total
screen width on any computer, what should its maximal pixel width be?

4. Obtain an image file and determine its dimensions in pixels. Add four different copies of it to a Web page, scaling it both up and down from its original
size. Be careful to preserve the aspect ratio during the scaling. Add some text
to your file, and then wrap this text so that it flows down the center, with
two copies of your image appearing on either side. Find a color that comple-
ments your image and add it as a background color.

5. Working with a photograph file, use a graphics editor to crop a very small
area from the original photograph. Save your cropped image in a new file
and display it on a Web page as a background pattern. Experiment with different cropped images until you find one that you like. How difficult was it
to find an image suitable for a background pattern?

CHAPTER FOUR

All About Hyperlinks

Text plus links equals hypertext. If we took the links away from the Web, it just wouldn't be the same. The mechanics of hyperlink creation are easy to learn, and the care and feeding of healthy hyperlinks is straightforward. Making appropriate design decisions for hyperlinks (such as when and how to insert them), however, requires having a feel for good user interface design. This chapter focuses primarily on the mechanics of hyperlinks and then closes with a quick overview of the link maintenance problem. Watch for useful hyperlink ideas in the tip boxes.

Chapter Objectives

- ☆ Introduce three types of hyperlinks
- ☆ Explain how to add absolute URLs
- ☆ Explain how to add relative URLs
- ☆ Explain how to add named anchors
- ☆ Examine the problem of link maintenance

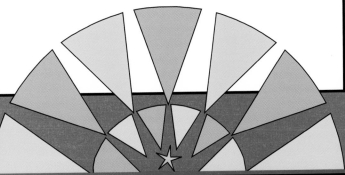

◎◎ Three Types of Hyperlinks

Using only a few formatting commands, you can create a simple Web page of text. It won't be hypertext, however, until you add hyperlinks. There are three types of HTML links, and each one is used in a different situation:

☆ **Absolute URL**: links to a page on a different Web server.

☆ **Relative URL**: links to a page on the same Web server.

☆ **Named anchor**: links to a different location on the same Web page.

Figure 4.1 illustrates the difference between relative and absolute URLs.

If you create a Web site of any complexity, you will need all three types of hyperlinks. They are not difficult to create, so there is no reason to be stingy with them. When you first look at a Web page, you can easily spot the "clickable text" where hyperlinks are lurking. Although all hyperlinks look alike in the browser's display window, you can determine the exact type of hyperlink found on the Web page by "pulling back the curtain" and examining the source file.

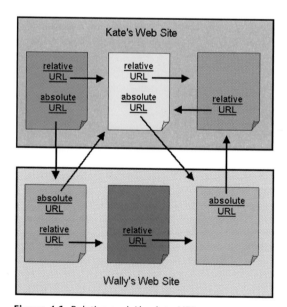

Figure 4.1 Relative and Absolute URLs

All hyperlinks have two components:

☆ A **link label** (a clickable element on a Web page)

☆ A **link destination** (a target destination)

The link label and the link destination are both components found inside the special HTML element used to create hyperlinks. We will look at this element in more detail shortly. For now, here's a sneak preview of a link in HTML:

```
<a href="http://www-edlab.cs.umass.edu/cs120/">CS120 Homepage</a>
```
Link destination   Link label

Armed with these two components, you can add any links needed to your Web pages. A *link label* can consist of any visible element on a Web page. Although it is usually text (clickable text), it can also be an image (a clickable image) or a table cell (Chapter Six introduces tables). A *link destination* is usually another `.html` file, but it can also be any file (not necessarily an `.html` file) that the Web page author has chosen to distribute over the Web.

☆**TIP**   **Never Use "Here" as a Link Label**

Always find appropriate phrases or text segments for your link labels, choosing descriptive labels that clearly identify your link destinations. Some search engines pay special attention to the link labels on your Web pages, using them to index your page more accurately. If necessary, rewrite your text to provide better link labels. The worst possible link label is the one that says "Click <u>here</u> to see ...".

◎◎ Absolute URLs

Suppose you want to add a link to a page that was written by a different author and is located on a different Web server. To set up such an *absolute URL*, you begin by selecting a label that will operate as the clickable link on your Web page. This label could be a segment of text embedded in a paragraph, an item in a bulleted list, or, if you want to create a clickable image, an entire IMG element. To create an absolute URL, you need to know two things:

☆ The complete URL for the site to which you want to link (the link destination)

☆ The position at which to insert the link on your own Web page (the link label)

For example, suppose that you are creating a Web page about tree houses. You want to create a link to a page that contains tree house construction plans. The tree house Web page has the following URL:

```
http://www.ekauria.net/construct/plans.html
```

This URL is the link destination. Before you can add it to your own Web page, however, you need to decide which visible part of the Web page will be the clickable link. Perhaps a sentence on your page mentions plans for tree houses. In particular, the phrase "building plan" would work well as a link label. You can then create the clickable link by inserting an **anchor element**, marked with the tag-pair <a></a>. First, place these tags so that they mark the beginning and the end of your link label. Next, add a *hypertext reference* (HREF) attribute inside the anchor tag and set it equal to the link destination (in double quotes). Figure 4.2 shows the complete anchor element for this example.

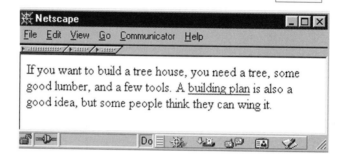

```
<p> If you want to build a tree house, you need a tree,
some good lumber, and a few tools. A <a href="http://
www.ekauria.net/construct/plans.html">building plan</a>
is also a good idea, but some
people think they can wing it.
```

Link label

Figure 4.2 A "Clickable Text" Link Label

☆**WARNING**　**Don't Forget the </a> Tag!**

When you use the anchor element, always be careful to close your link label with the </a> tag. If you omit this closing tag, your link label will extend throughout the remainder of your Web page, turning a large portion of your Web page into one gigantic hyperlink.

☆**TIP**　**Get Rid of That Blue Border**

If you use an IMG element as a link label, it will normally be displayed with a blue border (as seen in Figure 4.3). To see your image displayed without the blue border, set the BORDER attribute inside the IMG tag to 0.

Link labels for clickable text are typically displayed as blue text with blue underlining. If you prefer, you can customize your Web browser preference settings to produce a different color scheme.

You can create "clickable images" as easily as you create clickable text, but make sure your readers understand that they can click this link. Some images are self-explanatory. For example, many Web sites use a small icon of a house as a link back to the home page (see Figure 4.3).

```
<p> Even a well-constructed tree house will be stressed
by weather, by wear and tear, and by the very trees that
support it. If those trees are alive, they are growing
and shifting. To be safe, check your tree house for
signs of instability once a month.
</p>
<p>
<a href="home.html">
<img src="House.gif" width="50"
 height="55" alt="home icon">
</a>
```

Link label

Figure 4.3 A "Clickable Image" Link Label

Note how a little hand—the browser's mouse arrow—hovers over the lower-right corner of the clickable image icon. Whenever the mouse enters a clickable region, it changes from an arrow to a hand to signal the presence of a link. It will also display the contents of the ALT attribute, which can be a helpful place to explain the link to Web page visitors.

☆ **SHORTCUT** **Shortcut URLs**

Most Web servers support at least some standard address shortcuts. One frequently encountered shortcut is associated with files named index.html. Home pages are frequently named index .html so that visitors can reach them with the shortest possible URLs. If an index.html file appears in one of your Web file subdirectories, you can reference it in an absolute URL by simply omitting the filename portion of the URL. For example, http://www.umass.edu/news/ index.html and http://www.umass.edu/news/ are equivalent URLs.

That's all there is to creating an absolute URL hyperlink. As long as the URL in your link destination is current, and you can insert it into your HTML file without typos, it should be operational.

> ☆ **TIP** **Always Test Your Hyperlinks**
>
> Always check each link that you add to your Web pages to verify that it works correctly. To do so, display your page with a Web browser, and click each new link to test it. It is not enough to ensure that the link label looks good; you must also verify that the link destination is operational. Link testing is discussed in more detail at the end of this chapter.

◎◎ Relative URLs

When your Web site includes multiple Web pages, you can insert links to your own pages without specifying the full URLs for those pages. Instead of creating an absolute URL, you can use a shortcut address that consists of only the file's name and its location relative to the URL of the current Web page. For this reason, this type of hyperlink is called a *relative URL*.

The simplest relative URL connects two pages located in the same directory. Here's an example:

```
visit my <a href="booklist.html">recommended reading
list</a>
```

> ☆ **WARNING** **Relative Links Work Only at Home**
>
> If you examine the source code for someone else's Web site, you may find that these Web pages use relative URLs to reference other pages in that Web site. Those relative URLs will not work if you copy them and insert them into your own Web pages. To reference a Web page that is not your own, you must use an absolute URL. To find the correct link destination for an absolute URL, use your browser to visit the desired link destination, and then copy the URL in your Web browser's location window.

Relative URLs can be used only when the link destination resides on the same Web server as the page containing the link.

If your Web pages are located in different subdirectories, you can include additional path information in a relative URL. Chapter Three explained how browsers interpret path information for SRC attributes in IMG elements. The exact same rules apply to HREF attributes for relative URLs.

> ☆ **TIP** **Links Can Open New Browser Windows**
>
> To display the targets for your links in a new browser window, add a TARGET attribute inside the A tag with any quoted string value (for example, `<a target="window2">`). Some Web masters like to open all absolute URLs in a second browser window so that users will know when they've moved to another site (without completely leaving the old site, which remains available in the original browser window). Some users find it annoying when new browser windows pop up frequently, because these windows can proliferate and eventually need to be closed. If you decide to force new windows on your users, always use the same TARGET name to avoid creating multiple new browser windows.

When you create a link to another Web page on your own site, you have the option of using either a relative URL or an absolute URL. Although either option will work, it is considered better practice to use relative URLs when you are linking to your own in-site pages. This approach makes your Web pages *portable*. A Web page is **portable** if you can move it to a new Web server and all of its old links remain operational. Web page authors must occasionally switch Web servers. If the need to move your Web pages arises, you want to be able to install them on the new server with a minimal amount of work. If your in-site links are all absolute URLs, they will all point to the old server, and you must update them. If the links are all relative URLs, they will continue to work on the new Web server, as long as you meet two criteria:

☆ You move all of the pages on your site.

☆ You replicate your old directory structure on the new server.

You never know when you might need to move to a new Web server, so plan for an uncertain future and opt for relative URLs whenever possible.

☆ **TIP** **Some Absolute URLs Are Portable**

Absolute URLs to other Web sites are perfectly portable when you move your Web pages to a new Web server. It's only the absolute URLs to your own Web pages that must be updated when those pages are switched to a new server. This difference makes sense: any Web page that moves from one location to a new location will need a new URL. If a Web page at someone else's site moves, its absolute URL will need to be updated as well (though we'll describe a way to move a Web page without changing its absolute URL at the end of this chapter).

◎◎ Troubleshooting Broken Links

If you are testing your links and find one that generates an error message, work through the following checklist to pinpoint the problem. Some problems are easily fixed; others require action at the link's destination site. In the latter cases, all you can do is contact an administrator for the target site and inform him or her of the problem.

404-File Not Found: This error message indicates that the server name is valid, but the Web page could not be found at the specified location. Two things could be wrong.

First, the page might have moved. In this case, you can try to find its new location. Strip off the filename and see whether the resulting URL takes you to a related page. If it does, you might be able to navigate back to the desired page. If that step fails, strip off the next directory in the URL and test that address. With a little luck, one of the shorter URLs will produce a home page that you can use to locate the correct page.

Second, your URL might contain a typo. Visually inspect your URL for obvious problems. If nothing obvious strikes your eye, do the following:

☆ Look for uppercase/lowercase errors. Your path name and filename must duplicate the names on the Web server without any variations in the cases of the characters.

☆ Check for the letter "O" versus the number "0" and the letter "l" versus the number "1".

☆ Double-check the file extension. Is it `.html` or `.htm`? These extensions are not interchangeable.

☆ Make sure that you included `http://` if the link is supposed to be an absolute URL. If you leave out this preface, the browser may assume it is dealing with a relative URL and might conjure up a very strange URL when it tries to follow the link.

Server Not Found: Your URL contains a typo. Double-check the host name part of the URL.

Bad Request-No Address for Host: You are trying to access an absolute URL but your Internet connection is down.

Access Denied-File Permission Error: You cannot fix this problem unless you are the owner of the Web page (see Chapter Eight). Contact the site administrator for help.

◎◎ Named Anchors

A *named anchor* is a third type of hyperlink. In reality, a named anchor is really just a refinement of a Web page address. A link to a named anchor points to a fixed location within a particular Web page. Installing a link with a named anchor takes a little more work than creating links that use absolute or relative URLs. To create a named anchor, you mark the link destination on the target Web page so that a Web browser can find it (see Figure 4.4). This is done with a NAME attribute inside an anchor element. Let's demonstrate named anchors with an example.

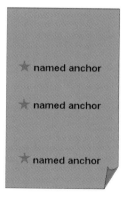

Figure 4.4 A Named Anchor Is a Location within a Web Page

> ☆ **TIP**   Named Anchors Belong on Long Web Pages
>
> Don't bother creating named anchors on a Web page if the page is so short that it can be viewed in a browser window without scrolling. Links to named anchors work only when pages can be scrolled.

Suppose you are designing an instructional Web page that contains several short subsections of text. You want to include a bulleted list at the top of the page that will operate as a clickable table of contents. You can accomplish this by turning each item on the list into a named anchor. Figure 4.5 shows the HTML source code for this kind of clickable table of contents.

```
<html>
<head>
<title> How to Build a Tree House </title>
</head>
<body>
<h1 align="center"> How to Build a Tree House</h1>
<p> If you want to build a tree house, you need:
<p>
<ul>
<li> <a href="#tree">a tree</a></li>
<li> <a href="#lumber">some good lumber</a></li>
<li> <a href="#tools">a few tools</a></li>
</ul>
<p>A construction plan is also a good idea but some peo-
ple think they can wing it.
<h3><a name="tree">A Tree</a></h3>
<p>Make sure the tree is large enough to support the
extra weight. Sometimes a stand of two or three trees
works nicely. If you distribute the weight over two or
three trees, smaller trees can be considered.
  .
  .
  .
<h3> <a name="lumber">Some Good Lumber</a></h3>
  .
  .
  .
<h3><a name="tools">A Few Tools</a></h3>
  .
  .
  .
</body>
</html>
```

Links to named anchors

Named anchors

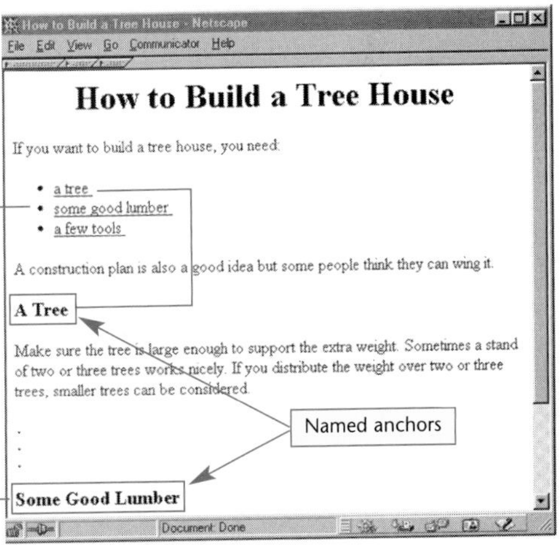

Figure 4.5 A Clickable Table of Contents with Named Anchors

A link to a named anchor on the current Web page uses the anchor element with an HREF attribute for its link destination, just like absolute and relative URLs. Instead of specifying a URL or a filename as the link destination, however, you specify a named anchor. Thus a named anchor is simply an anchor element with a NAME attribute. The value for the NAME attribute is a quoted string (for example, `<a name="tree">`). To reference a named anchor in an HREF attribute, you use the same name as the NAME attribute, but alert the Web browser that it is a named anchor rather than a relative URL. Web browsers recognize a named anchor because of the pound (#) character at the beginning of the anchor name (for example, `<a href="#tree">`).

Named anchors help Web page visitors move through large text documents in a nonlinear fashion. When creating a clickable table of contents, you should insert additional links at the end of each target segment to return users to the table of contents. A link to a named anchor can jump people back up to the top of a page as easily as forward links jump down. Such return links are usually labeled "Back to Top." Good Web page design includes anticipating all of the directions in which a Web page visitor might want to go and making that navigation as easy as possible.

☆TIP   Named Anchors in Relative and Absolute URLS

You can create a link to a specific location on any Web page that contains a named anchor at that location. To jump to a specific location on a different Web page, just append the anchor name (including the # character) to the end of the relative URL or the absolute URL. For example,

```
http://www-edlab.cs.umass.edu/cs120/index.html#students
```

takes visitors to a point about halfway down that particular Web page.

Named anchors are typically used to help people "hop around" the same Web page. In such cases, the author of the "hopping link" is the author of the Web page, and he or she can insert a named anchor in any location requiring a destination for a hop. If you are familiar with a Web page that uses named anchors, you can take advantage of them in creating your own links. For example, to link to a specific location on someone else's Web page, simply examine the source code for that page to find the name of the anchor, then add it to an absolute URL on your own page.

☆TIP   Other Authors' Anchors

You can use a named anchor on someone else's Web page to link to a specific location within the target page. But be careful: you have no control over any named anchors that are not yours, and the other Web page author might rearrange his or her anchors without warning. For this reason, you may prefer to use absolute links without any anchors. You can always offer instructions nearby that describe how users can reach a specific destination. That way you can point people to the right neighborhood, but then trust them to navigate the site once they get there.

Table 4.1 summarizes the most important anchor attributes.

Table 4.1 Selected Frames-Related Attributes

HTML Element	Attributes	Attribute Values	What the Attribute Does
`<a></a>` (anchor)	`href=`	[an absolute URL or a relative URL]	Specifies the link destination for a hyperlink.
	`name=`	[any string]	Creates a named anchor in a Web page.
	`target=`	[any string]	Activates a named browser window.

Testing Your Hyperlinks

Nonworking links can frustrate Web site visitors, so keep your Web page in good operating condition by periodically verifying that all links still work correctly. It is not enough to know that a link was working when you first created it. After all, a link that works today might not work tomorrow. The page might be removed from the Web or the page's author might rearrange some files or directories, rendering the old URL obsolete. Ongoing maintenance is needed to ensure that hyperlinks remain operational next week, next month, and next year. This requirement is one of the hidden costs associated with posting pages on the Web. Although it is certainly fun to create new Web pages, most people find maintaining existing pages to be tedious.

If your Web page contains only 5 to 10 links, you can check them manually every week or two and still keep your site in tip-top shape. Unfortunately, manual link checking soon becomes onerous, even for a small number of links. If you forgo this routine, your site will suffer and your users will feel neglected or annoyed—and may never return. If your site is compelling and entertaining, your users may forgive you. Most of us can't count on such a loyal and understanding following, so it's important to keep all of your Web page links operational and current.

☆ **TIP   Can Links Be Tested without the Internet?**

If you maintain a copy of your Web site on a local computer for ongoing development, you can test your relative URLs and links to local named anchors from your local host, without Internet access. In contrast, you must have an active Internet connection to test absolute URLs pointing to other Web sites.

An **automated link checker** is a utility that takes much of the drudgery out of ongoing link maintenance. If you have a moderately large Web site with more than 100 links and you care about your visitors, you absolutely must use a link checker. You have two options in that case.

The easiest solution is to use an application service provider (ASP). An ASP is a commercial service that offers Web-based computing capabilities to its subscribers. An ASP that offers a link validation service uses its own link checker to analyze your Web site and produce link reports on a weekly or monthly basis. You won't have to remember to check your links—the service will remember for you. You simply read the reports and fix any stale (that is, broken) links. Although these commercial services work quite well, you must continue to pay for them as long as you use them, which could be indefinitely.

If you want to cap your maintenance expenses, you can install your own link checker and run link checks yourself. Many link checkers are available on the Web. A few are distributed at no cost, and others are free to use during a trial examination period. The most sophisticated products are geared toward professional site administrators (for example, *Watchfire's Linkbot Personal Edition* retails for $295) and offer sophisticated features for comprehensive site administration. Figure 4.6 shows a more moderately priced under $40) link checker named *LinkRunner*.

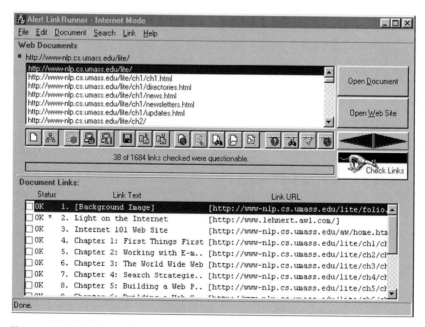

Figure 4.6 A LinkRunner Status Report

Of course, you cannot automate every aspect of hyperlink maintenance. A link checker simply brings problems to your attention; it doesn't fix them. A good link checker will produce a report summarizing all possible problems found on your site (see Figure 4.7). For each link that is flagged as questionable or broken, you must then decide how to proceed. You might need to find a new URL for the original resource, or you might need to remove the reference altogether. In either case, some updating of the Web page will be necessary—and only you can ultimately decide how to handle each link that requires attention.

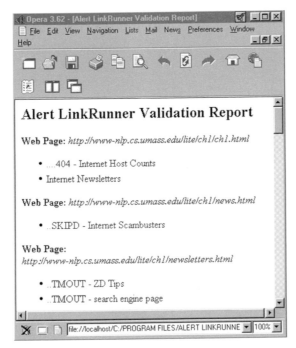

Figure 4.7 LinkRunner Displays All Problem Links with Error Messages

A good link checker will be easy to use and require a minimal amount of study and preparation. All you will need to specify is the location of the Web site to be checked. You can do so by specifying a directory location on the Web server or by listing specific URLs individually. The link checker then collects all of the hyperlinks in the target documents and sends out requests to all of the servers that are hosting targeted links. If a server replies with a valid Web page, the link to that server passes the test. If it returns an error message, the link is added to the list of problem links. A good link checker will also associate an error code with each problem link (see Figure 4.8).

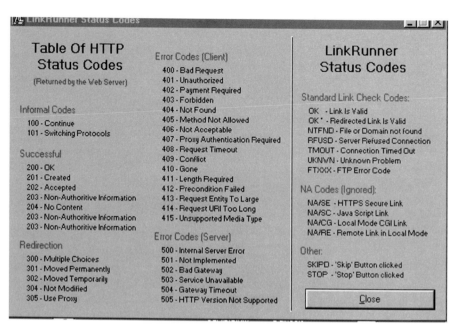

Figure 4.8 Links Can Fail in Many Ways

☆**TIP**   **Control Your Own Domain Name**

To ensure that links to your Web pages always stay healthy, even if you switch Web servers, you can obtain your own domain name. To get a domain name, you must first find a domain name that no one else has claimed, and then you must register that name to ensure that no one else can use it. Many commercial services are available to help you register a domain name (see the list of URLs at the end of this chapter). Registration fees typically range from $30 to $50 per year.

Once you have your own domain name, you can subscribe to a **virtual domain hosting service**, usually through an Internet service provider (ISP). This service allows you to obtain space on a Web server under your personal domain name. For example, if the author owns the domain name `wlehnert.com`, then she can install her Web pages on a Web server so that people can find those pages under URLs that begin with `http://www.wlehnert.com/`, even though the server might have a different host name. By using a virtual domain name, you can make sure that your Web pages are always available under permanent URLs, even if you change ISPs. ISPs normally charge for this service, with monthly hosting fees on top of the yearly registration fee for the domain name itself.

Although you might have to pay for a good link checker, the investment is worthwhile if you want to keep your Web pages healthy and up-to-date. Some link failures are transient and will disappear if you wait 24 hours; others are permanent. By minimizing the amount of time that you spend on routine maintenance, you'll have more time and energy to devote to creative enhancements and major overhauls of your Web pages. Link maintenance is one of the more tedious responsibilities associated with Web sites, but the importance of frequent link checking cannot be overestimated. A site whose links are always operational will be greatly appreciated and is likely to win a loyal following.

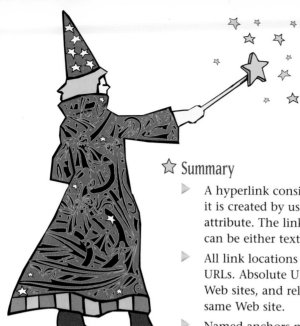

☆ Summary

▷ A hyperlink consists of a link label and a link destination; it is created by using the `<a></a>` tag-pair with an HREF attribute. The link label is the clickable part of the link; it can be either text or an image.

▷ All link locations are specified as either absolute or relative URLs. Absolute URLs are needed for Web pages at other Web sites, and relative URLs are used for Web pages in the same Web site.

▷ Named anchors make it possible to link to specific locations within a long Web page. They can be added to both absolute and relative URLs.

▷ All absolute links should be periodically tested to verify that they work correctly. A link checker streamlines the tedious process of checking all the links for a large Web site.

☆ Online References

Using Relative URLs
`http://www.stack.nl/%7Egalactus/html/urls.html`

Web Structure
`http://www.matcmp.sunynassau.edu/~glassr/html/url.htm`

Troubleshooting Broken Image Links (and Hyperlinks)
`http://www.hostingmanual.net/forum/Support/12.shtml`

Alert LinkRunner
`http://www.alertbookmarks.com/lr/`

LinkAlarm Web Service for Eliminating Broken Links
`http://www.linkalarm.com/`

Network Solutions WHOIS (domain name look up)
`http://networksolutions.com/cgi-bin/whois/whois`

TopHosts.com-The Complete Web Hosting Resource
`http://www.TopHosts.com/`

☆ Review Questions

1. Which HTML element and element attribute is used for setting up link destinations?

2. How do an absolute URL and a relative URL differ?

3. Suppose you are working on a Web page, and you notice that the last paragraph of your page has somehow become one huge hyperlink. How could this problem happen, and how can you fix it?

4. When do you have the option of using either absolute or relative URLs?

5. What does it mean for a Web site to be portable? How can you make sure that the pages on your Web site are portable?

6. If you were to copy an `.html` file from someone else's Web page and add it to your own Web site, some of the hyperlinks on this page might not work anymore. Why might this problem occur, and how could you fix it? (*Note*: If you actually published a copy of someone else's Web page without obtaining that author's permission, you could be sued for copyright infringement.)

7. Which HTML element and element attribute are used to set up named anchors?

8. How does a browser know when it is looking at a link to a named anchor?

9. Ongoing link maintenance is an unavoidable fact of life for Web masters. Is it possible to have a Web site that contains lots of links but does not require periodic link checks to keep all links healthy all the time? Explain your reasoning.

10. How does virtual domain hosting help prevent hyperlink errors?

☆ Hands-On Exercises

1. The URL for CNet's news page is `http://news.cnet.com/`. Create a Web page with a link to CNet that looks like this:

   > Daily news of interest to computer professionals can be found at <u>CNet's Tech News page</u>.

   Test your link to verify that it operates correctly.

2. Using an image file of your choice, insert a scaled-down version of the image on a Web page. Make sure that the image is being displayed correctly before you continue. Next, turn this little image into a link label for a relative link that points to the original image file. When you click on the smaller version of the image, your browser should display the original image file without any scaling. Once your clickable image is working, modify it to eliminate the blue border around the clickable image.

3. Create a link to a page of your choice (you could use the link from Exercise 1 or 2) and modify it so that your target page appears in a new browser window.

4. Copy the code from Figure 4.5 into an `.html` file and test the named anchor links to verify that they are working properly. Your page must be scrollable for the links to be operational. (*Note*: Making your browser window smaller is easier than typing in a lot of text to take up space.) Once you have the links working, add three new links that will return users to the top of the current page. Insert these new links at the end of "tree," "lumber," and "tools" sections, enabling readers to easily navigate this page no matter where they are.

5. Create an `.html` file that contains a relative link to a `.txt` file (either new or existing) on your own local host. The text file does not need to be in the same subdirectory if you want to add path information to your link. When the link is working, your browser should display the `.txt` file. What does the `.txt` file look like? Try linking to another file on your hard drive (pick a file type other than `.html`, `.htm`, `.gif`, or `.jpg`). What happens when you click on a link to some other file type?

CHAPTER FIVE

WORKING WITH IMAGES

P eople are visual creatures. We are naturally attracted to colors, images, and graphical representations of all sorts of information. On the Web, a picture may be worth a thousand words—but only if it doesn't take too long to download. When it comes to computer graphics, a little know-how can make a big difference to your Web pages. With just a bit of extra effort, you can prepare images for your Web pages that are both attractive and bandwidth-sensitive. Plus, working with image files is a lot of fun! Whether you create your own artwork and photographs or utilize free resources found on the Web, you'll find it gratifying to personalize your Web pages with hand-picked images, icons, buttons, and navigation menus.

Chapter Objectives

☆ Explain when to employ the GIF, JPEG, and PNG file formats

☆ Show how thumbnail previews can minimize bandwidth consumption

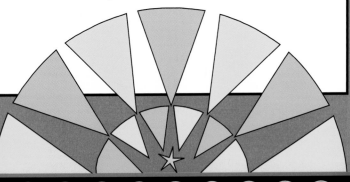

☆ Find out how to create and use transparent GIFs

☆ Demonstrate how to create an image map

☆ Introduce animated GIFs and streaming media

◉◎ Image File Formats

All artwork and photographs found on the Web are stored in binary files. These files reside on Web servers along with the HTML files that refer to them. You can obtain graphics for your Web pages in many ways, including finding clip art on the Web, taking photographs with digital cameras, using scanners to digitize images, and working with software for artists (or adventurous amateurs).

GIF and JPEG Files

Two file formats are commonly used for Web page graphics: the GIF format and the JPEG (or just JPG) format. **GIF** (**Graphics Interchange Format**) files are best for line art, cartoons, and simple images. In contrast, **JPEG** (**Joint Photographic Experts Group**) files are better-suited to photographs and artwork that include many colors and fine gradations in color. Each format works better for certain kinds of images because of the unique way in which it stores images.

> ☆WARNING   BITMAP (.BMP) Files Do Not Belong on the Web
>
> While using Internet Explorer, you might stumble upon an image-related feature that is somewhat misleading. Namely, Internet Explorer displays .BMP (BITMAP) files. Although you might be tempted to add a .BMP file to a Web page, you should resist this urge for two reasons. First, other Web browsers do not display .BMP files. Second, .BMP files tend to be approximately 10 times larger than their JPEG and GIF equivalents. *Never add a BITMAP file to a Web page.*

JPEG files use a 24-bit color palette (as described in Chapter Three). Color photographs are often stored as JPEG files because the 24-bit palette is large enough to cover all possible colors needed for color photography. By comparison, GIF images use an 8-bit color palette, which means that each GIF image is constructed from 256 possible colors. If you save a photograph as a GIF file, the format may not provide enough colors to cover all those needed, so some colors will be created by *dithering*. In a **dithered color**, pixels of other colors are mixed to create the illusion of a color that's not actually part of the available color palette. For example, if you were missing a certain shade of green, you could dither a pattern of blue pixels and yellow pixels to create a region that looks green.

> ☆TIP   True or False: All GIF Files Are Patented
>
> The GIF file format uses an adaptation of the Lempel Ziv Welch (LZW) algorithm for image compression. The LZW algorithm is patented by Unisys, which charges a licensing fee to commercial developers of GIF-based software but allows all end users and non-commercial software developers to use GIF files without restriction. Considerable controversy and confusion arose regarding Unisys's patent and its implications for Web page authors during the 1990s, but those questions have since been resolved. If you are not a professional programmer, the GIF controversy does not concern you.

Many photographs can be saved in the GIF format and still be visually indistinguishable from their JPEG counterparts. In other cases, however, a loss of tone and detail becomes apparent when you compare images saved in the two formats side by side. Figure 5.1 compares a landscape in JPEG format with the same image in GIF format. Notice how much detail and texture has been lost in the sky in going from JPEG to GIF.

Figure 5.1 JPEG (above) and GIF (below) Renderings of a Photograph

Whereas all JPEG images rely on the same 24-bit color palette, each GIF image can use its own customized palette of 256 (8-bit) colors. When you convert an image to the GIF format, a frequency analysis of the image's colors identifies the most commonly used colors and produces a reduced color palette—known as an **adaptive palette**—based on that analysis. Figure 5.2 shows a GIF rendering of a photograph along with its color palette (as displayed by Softkey's PhotoFinish 4).

Figure 5.3 shows another photograph with a different color palette. In many cases, 256 colors provide adequate coverage for photographs. When coverage falls short, you will see degradations in texture, shadings, and details associated with subtle color shifts.

Figure 5.2 An Eight-Bit (256-Color) Palette with Mostly Greens

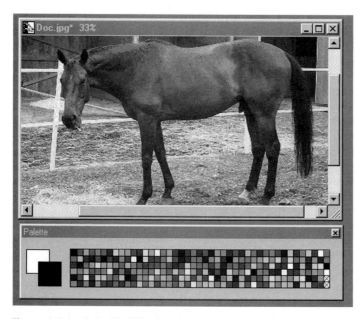

Figure 5.3 An Eight-Bit (256-Color) Palette with Mostly Browns and Grays

GIF images are especially well suited for artwork and designs containing large regions that are filled in by a single color, with clean boundaries separating the color regions. For example, text images, logos, cartoons, and line drawings are all excellent candidates for GIF renderings. Figure 5.4 shows how the same graphic design is rendered in both GIF and JPEG formats.

Figure 5.4 GIF (left) and JPEG (right) Renderings of a Graphic Design

The noise in the JPEG version is called **ghosting** and results in a blurry-looking graphic. Not only is the JPEG image inferior to the corresponding GIF image, but JPEG renderings of artwork can consume 10 times as much memory as their GIF counterparts do.

☆**TIP**   **Think Small**

Keep graphics files as small as possible when you are putting them on the Web, because smaller files translate into faster Web page downloads. As a rule of thumb, try to use image files that are no larger than 40KB. Choose between GIF or JPEG files based on the type of image. When it comes to the GIF-versus-JPEG battle, the best image quality generally goes hand-in-hand with smaller files, so choosing the right image format is really a win-win scenario.

Image Compression

Image compression refers to a process by which the memory requirements of an image file become reduced. Some image representations work better with certain compression techniques, and particular compression techniques are often built into file formats. For example, a variant on LZW compression is part of the GIF file format. In a **lossy** image format, the compression technique trades off image quality in exchange for greater memory savings. The GIF file format is not lossy (at least, not after the image is rendered in 8-bit color). In contrast, the JPEG format is lossy, which makes it very useful for the Web. Software tools that save images in JPEG format typically allow users to control the amount of compression applied to the image, which means that Web page authors can manage the trade-off between file size and image quality.

Images can withstand different amounts of compression without sacrificing too much degradation in quality. Although achieving an additional reduction in file size might warrant some amount of image degradation, eventually the image will become unacceptable. Figure 5.5 shows how a 38KB JPEG photograph (upper left) can be saved with varying degrees of file compression and image degradation. You can compress this particular image to a 10KB file (upper right) without serious degradation, but rapid deterioration is evident with 5KB (lower left) and 4KB (lower right) files.

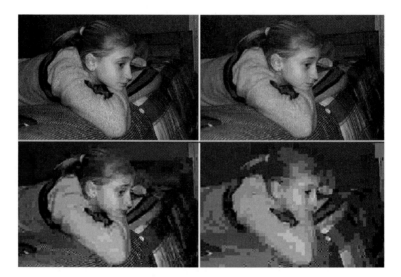

Figure 5.5 Lossy File Compression

At first glance, the difference between a 10KB file and a 38KB file might not seem terribly significant. If your Web page contained 10 such images, however, the difference between 100KB and 380KB could mean that some visitors stay to see your site whereas others leave before they see everything. Whenever you can cut your Web page download time by 50% or more, the exercise is generally worth the effort.

Interlaced GIFs

To make slow downloads less annoying, you can use interlaced GIFs on your Web pages. An **interlaced GIF** file produces its displays in four passes (see Figure 5.6). The first pass produces an image based on every tenth line of pixels. On the second pass, the display shows every fifth line. On the third pass, every other line is filled in. On the fourth pass, the complete image is displayed. Incremental graphic displays can be interesting to watch and will pacify all but the most harried Web users.

Figure 5.6 An Interlaced GIF Becomes Visible in Stages

You can convert any GIF file to an interlaced GIF file, provided that the original file conforms to the GIF89 formatting standard (the norm). Many file utilities and GIF converters support an interlaced GIF option, which you can select when you save the image to a file. In addition, you can achieve a similar effect with **progressive JPEG** files.

☆**TIP** **The PNG File Format**

The PNG (Portable Networks Graphics) file format was created (at least in part) in response to patent complications surrounding the GIF file format. When GIF's future seemed uncertain, programmers decided to create an improved file format that could be used in place of the GIF format. PNG files are comparable to GIF files in terms of compression (in fact, they tend to be 5% to 25% smaller than GIF files), and they are lossless. PNG files can be interlaced-, and support transparency, just like GIF files. Unlike GIF, however, PNG does not support animation. (We will discuss transparency and animation later in this chapter.)

◎◎ Thumbnail Previews

When you can't avoid including a large image file on your Web page and don't want to burden your visitors with long download times, you should let each visitor decide whether the wait is worth the end result. The standard way to provide this service is with a thumbnail preview. A **thumbnail preview** (also called a **thumbnail sketch**) is a clickable, bandwidth-efficient version of a larger graphic that contains a link to the original image. Visitors can request the original version by clicking the thumbnail preview.

Your Web page should include some instructions that explain how the thumbnail preview works—after all, some people are in the habit of clicking everything on a page just to see what happens. If you make the thumbnail's image very small, experienced Web users will probably understand what's going on. Nevertheless, it doesn't hurt to explain the process. Figure 5.7 shows an HTML link label and link destination for a thumbnail preview. Note that the HTML code does not include WIDTH and HEIGHT attributes for the link destination. When a Web browser displays an image file directly (as the value of an HREF attribute), it always uses the original dimensions of the image. That is, you cannot scale an image that does not appear inside an HTML file.

```
<a href="meteor.jpg"> ─────────  This link destination is a 96KB file.
    <img src="meteor-sm.jpg" width="91" height="67">
</a>
Click on this picture
to see the original (96KB).   This link label is a "clickable" 9KB
                               version of the original 96KB file.
```

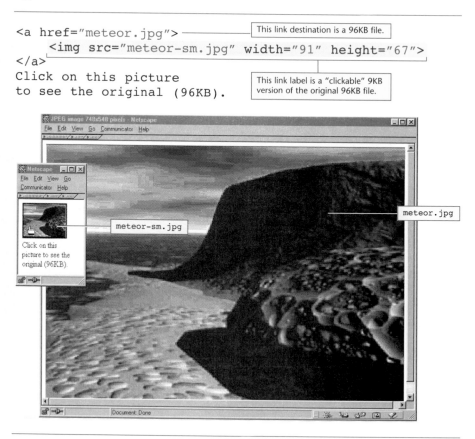

Figure 5.7 A Thumbnail Preview

You can use a graphics editor to create a compressed version of the original image file for your thumbnail preview. If you simply shrink the original image by using smaller WIDTH and HEIGHT attributes, visitors will begin downloading the original file even as they are viewing a scaled-down version of it. Of course, this process defeats the whole purpose of the thumbnail preview. The best option is to save your thumbnail as a JPEG image, which enables you to control the amount of compression applied to the image. A large image can be maximally compressed to the lowest quality level and still work for a thumbnail preview. Remember, your goal is to minimize bandwidth requirements, not to preserve the image quality. Most graphics editors and image conversion applications will give you an opportunity to apply variable degrees of compression when you save a JPEG file. If no compression option pops up automatically while you are executing a SaveAs command, look for a preference setting that controls the amount of compression (see Figure 5.8).

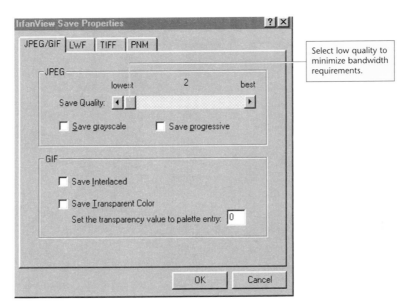

Figure 5.8 Thumbnail Previews Should be Minimal-Quality Images

> ☆ **TIP**   **Describe File Sizes**
>
> When you offer a link to a large image file, include the size of the file (as in Figure 5.7, for example). Users can then decide for themselves whether to start the download.

You don't have to use thumbnail previews to give visitors control over large downloads. In fact, you can use any text link to point to a large image. The important point is to minimize the bandwidth requirements of your mandatory Web page downloads. Isolate all large image files from your main Web pages so they can be accessed, but only on demand.

⊚⊚ Transparent GIFs

A **transparent GIF** looks as if the image were drawn directly on your Web page. That is, it allows your Web page's background color or background pattern to show through those portions of the image that have been designated as transparent. Figure 5.9 shows a version of the same Web page depicted in Figure 3.11; in Figure 5.9, the two images have been made transparent so that the yellow background shows through the background of both the photograph and the drawing. Note that the original woodcut drawing had a white background, but the new version takes on the background color of the Web page.

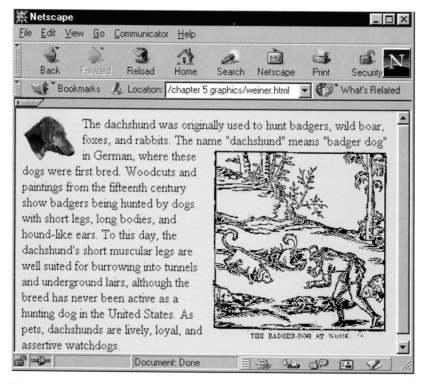

Figure 5.9 Two Transparent GIFs over a Yellow Background

To create a transparent GIF, you first identify which portion of the image will serve as the designated background. Then, whenever that image appears on a Web page, its background region behaves as if it were transparent, inheriting the background color (or background pattern) of the Web page beneath it. Transparency works well with images that have clearly defined backgrounds, such as line art and cartoons.

Alternatively, black-and-white line drawings can be rendered as "virtual stencils" if you want to make the foreground (rather than the background) transparent. In Figure 5.10, the same transparent GIF is displayed against three different background colors. Here the foreground of the drawing is transparent, so it picks up the color of the background like a stencil. In Chapter Six, you will see how to set up Web page layouts with different colored backgrounds when you learn about tables.

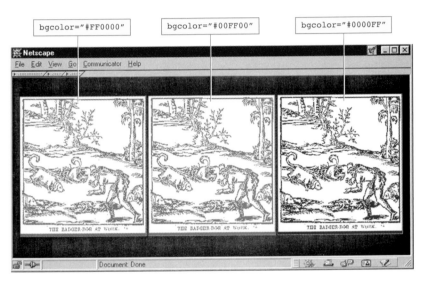

Figure 5.10 A Transparent Foreground Behaves Like a Stencil

To turn a photograph into a transparent GIF, you must do a little tinkering with a graphics editor. The trick is to make the background of the image become one solid color without speckles or streaks. No matter how uniform their backgrounds may look from a distance, photographs always contain some stray pixels of different colors that must be cleaned up to achieve an effective transparency. In Figure 5.11, a large photograph is initially cropped to a head shot and then edited to replace the background with a solid color (using a paintbrush tool and a zoom-in feature for editing the boundary pixels with greater precision). Once the background has been carefully cleaned up, the image is transformed into a transparent GIF with a transparentizing tool.

Many graphics editors can convert GIF images into transparent GIFs. You can also download utilities from the Web for this purpose (see Figure 5.12).

Once you have created a transparent GIF, you can experiment with background colors until you find one that works well with the image. Transparent GIFs are often used for buttons and navigational icons as well as larger pieces of artwork on a Web page. Indeed, including a few small transparent GIFs can dress up a Web site without overpowering it.

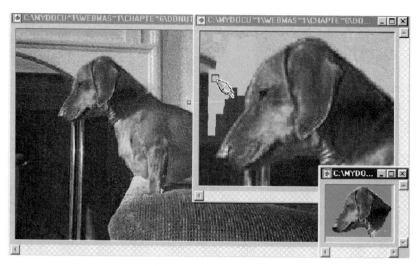

Figure 5.11 Transparent Photographs Require Extra Work

☆ **WARNING Pick Your Background Color Carefully**

For the background of a photograph, pick a color that does not occur elsewhere in the picture. If this color occurs in places other than the background, those pixels will be made transparent as well.

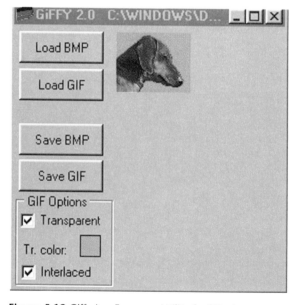

Figure 5.12 Giffy Is a Freeware Utility for Windows

☆ **WARNING** **Interlacing and Transparency**

If you use one file utility to create an interlaced GIF file and another utility to make the same GIF become transparent, be careful to interlace the image first, before making it transparent. Otherwise, your image might show some gray ghosts on your Web page.

◎◎ Image Maps

The best Web sites are easy to navigate. In fact, an eye-catching navigational menu is a hallmark of a well-designed Web site. Navigational menus are constructed from image maps and are typically used in conjunction with frames. This section describes how to create image maps, and Chapter Seven covers the use of frames.

Anyone who has spent five minutes on the Web has seen an image map in action. An **image map** is an image on a Web page that has been divided into regions called hotzones. Each **hotzone** is a clickable region associated with a link destination. The user clicks his or her mouse anywhere within a hotzone to follow the link associated with that hotzone. Thus image maps with hotzones offer another way of adding hyperlinks to a Web page. Using multiple hotzones, you can specify more than one hyperlink per image so that different parts of the image correspond to different hyperlinks. For example, Figure 5.13 shows a GIF image of a button panel that lends itself to an image map. Each of the six buttons corresponds to a separate hotzone.

In the early days of the Web, image maps required a program called a **server-side image map** that ran on the Web server. Today, most image maps are handled by Web browsers; these maps are called **client-side image maps**. Client-side image maps first became popular in 1997, when HTML 3.2 was released and provided a MAP tag. These maps are superior to server-side image maps because they operate independently on the user's computer without additional browser-server interactions. This approach minimizes bandwidth consumption and makes the map work much more quickly.

Figure 5.13 A Button Panel for an Image Map

Many image maps are designed to dynamically change in appearance when a mouse rolls over a hotzone. For example, a button might light up or change colors when the mouse enters the button's region. To learn how to create such a dynamic image map, consult a JavaScript tutorial that explains how to add *mouseovers* to image maps. This book covers only clickable image maps.

☆**TIP**   **Avoid Hidden Hotzones**

When you select an image for an image map, pick one that is intuitively obvious. Your user should be able to glance at the image and immediately understand that it is a place to point and click. You can always hide a hotzone in an image where no one expects it. Doing so will only annoy people, however, unless the site is designed to be a puzzle of some sort.

To create a clickable image map, you must mark each clickable region within the image using x-y coordinate notation. This coordinate system might seem somewhat confusing at first, because the y-axis is *positive* beneath the x-axis (not negative, as in the Cartesian coordinate system you've seen in math classes). In the coordinate system for an image map, y-values increase as you move *down* the axis (in math notation, y-values increase as you move *up* the axis). After inverting the y-axis, you simply use standard coordinate geometry to mark the hotzones. In particular, you represent a rectangular region by specifying two items: the coordinate pair of the rectangle's upper-left corner and the coordinate pair of the rectangle's lower-right corner (see Figure 5.14).

The ISMAP Trick

Using Navigator or Internet Explorer, you can view any image and see the x-y coordinates for any spot in the image by positioning your cursor on the spot. Follow these steps:

1. Set up an `IMG` tag with an `ISMAP` attribute, and make it a link label for an A tag. Here is an example:

   ```
   <a href="placeholder.html"><img src="test.jpg" ismap>
   </a>
   ```

2. Replace `test.jpg` with the filename for the image that you want to map. Don't worry if the file `placeholder.html` doesn't exist—you never actually visit this link destination while carrying out the `ISMAP` trick.

3. Display the HTML file that contains this link with a Web browser, and look at your image.

4. Place your cursor inside the image, and look at the status message at the bottom of the browser window. At the end of the filename are two numbers separated by a comma—the x-y coordinates for the current cursor position (see Figure 5.14). (If the toolbar obscures your view of the status message, enlarge the browser window.)

Suppose you want to create an image map for the navigational menu shown in Figure 5.13. The image file contains six buttons, so you need a separate hotzone for each button. Start by collecting the x-y coordinates for the upper-left and lower-right corners of each button. Next, use the `MAP` tag to create the actual image map. The `MAP` tag allows you to identify multiple hotzones within a single image by specifying a separate `AREA` tag for each hotzone. The AREA tag's attributes describe

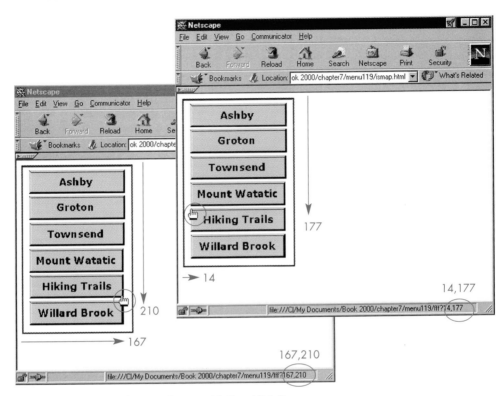

Figure 5.14 Locating x-y Coordinates with Your Web Browser

Before you start collecting coordinate pairs for your image, make sure that the image is the same size it will be on your Web page. If you must scale your image by using WIDTH and HEIGHT attributes on your Web page, take a screen shot of the image as it appears in your browser window and then work with that version as you map the regions of the image. If you map an image that is larger or smaller than the version found on your final Web page, your hotzones will be unusable because the designated link locations won't map correctly to the coordinates of the image being displayed.

the hotzone's shape and location. The SHAPE attribute allows you to specify a rectangle, and the COORDS attribute identifies the location using coordinate pairs. For example, in coords="x_1,y_1,x_2,y_2", (x_1, y_1) are the coordinates for the upper-left corner of the rectangular hotzone and (x_2, y_2) are the coordinates for the lower-right corner. You also need an HREF attribute to specify the link destination for each hotzone. The resulting image map follows:

```
<map name="menumap">
 <area shape=rect coords="14,5,168,42" href="ashby.html">
 <area shape=rect coords="15,46,171,88"
    href="groton.html">
 <area shape=rect coords="13,89,170,124"
    href="townsend.html">
 <area shape=rect coords="13,131,170,166"
    href="watatic.html">
 <area shape=rect coords="14,174,170,209"
    href="hiking.html">
 <area shape=rect coords="14,215,167,252"
    href="willard.html">
</map>
```

This MAP element must be added to the BODY of the Web page, and the attribute `usemap="#menumap"` must be added to the IMG element of the image being mapped:

```
<img border=0 src="fullmap.gif" width="181" height="267"
 usemap="#menumap">
```

Note that these coordinates don't have to line up perfectly with the buttons on the image. Users won't know or care if the hotzones are off by a few pixels.

A Six-Step Image Map

To create an image map, follow these steps:

1. Start with an image file (GIF or JPEG—it doesn't matter which).

2. View the image with your Web browser using the ISMAP trick.

3. Record the coordinate pairs for each rectangular hotzone.

4. Create an AREA tag for each hotzone, and place each AREA tag inside a MAP tag.

5. Add the MAP tag to the BODY of the Web page (it doesn't matter where).

6. Add a USEMAP attribute to the IMG tag for the image just mapped.

As you have just seen, it is easy to create image maps with rectangular hotzones by hand, using only a Web browser and the ISMAP trick. Unfortunately, this approach becomes tedious when you must add numerous image maps. If you expect to create many image maps or if you need to work with nonrectangular hotzones, you should use an image mapper. An **image mapper** is a software utility that generates a MAP element using regions identified by point-and-drag mouse operations. Figure 5.15 shows the image mapper in Dreamweaver marking a hotzone. Table 5.1 describes selected HTML attributes related to image mapping.

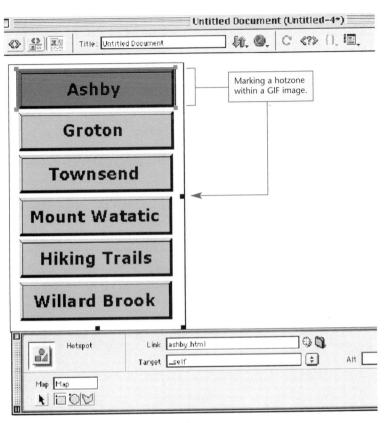

Figure 5.15 Dreamweaver's Image Mapper

Table 5.1 Selected Image Mapping Attributes

HTML Element	Attributes	Attribute Values	What the Attribute Does
`<area>`	`coords=`	[two coordinate pairs for rectangles]	Specifies the location and size of the hotzone
	`href=`	[an absolute URL or a relative URL]	Specifies the link destination for the hotzone
	`shape=`	`RECT` for rectangles	Specifies the shape of the hotzone
`<map></map>`	`name=`	[any string]	Names the image map

◎◎ Animation and Streaming Media

You can easily add cartoon animations to your Web pages. The GIF file format supports a limited form of animation known as an *animated GIF*. An animated GIF comprises a collection of GIF images that are viewed like the individual frames of a movie reel, typically set up with a 20-millisecond delay between each frame (although the actual delay experienced will depend on the speed of the computer displaying the animation). You handle animated GIF files just like any other GIF file. These files share the same file extension as nonanimated GIF files. Likewise, they are added to a Web page using the SRC attribute for an IMG element, just like any other GIF. You can add animations to your Web pages by including files found in animation libraries, or you can create your own animated GIFs. Figure 5.16 shows a few frames from a 19-frame animated GIF of a running puma.

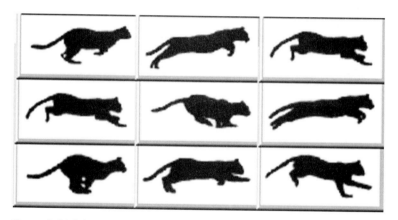

Figure 5.16 Selected Frames from a 19-Frame Animated GIF

Many software options to generate animations on Web pages exist. In addition, home computers can now be configured with enough memory and bandwidth, as well as the appropriate software bundles, to operate as affordable video production studios. Posting complicated animations and video clips (mini-movies) on a Web page requires using some special tricks, however, reflecting the bandwidth-intensive nature of the files involved.

Video and audio files are usually made available as streaming media. **Streaming media** is a technology that makes it possible to play large multimedia files in real time while the files continue to download.

When you download a streaming audio file, your video (or audio) player starts to save the front end of the file in a temporary holding area, called a **buffer**. The player does not begin to play the file, however, until a suitable portion of that file has been saved to the buffer. Once enough data have been buffered, the player begins to play it, even as it continues to download and save the rest of the file. Buffer space is recycled whenever possible, ensuring that room for more data is always available. Ideally, the player should never process its data more quickly than the Internet connection can fill the buffer. If the player does get ahead of the buffer, a break in the video display will occur and you must wait for the video to restart. Allocating a suitably large enough buffer can usually smooth out the variations in throughput that might otherwise interfere with a real-time rendering of the data.

Implementing streaming media on the Web requires the use of special software by both the Web page author and the Web page visitor. For example, animations created with Macromedia Flash require the use of the Macromedia Shockwave plug-in. Although the most popular Web browsers now install Shockwave automatically, some people will inevitably lack the right browser configurations to view cutting-edge Shockwave animations. The most recent technologies always dance on the "bleeding edge" of Web page design. If you want to play it safe, stick to animated GIFs. Then again, by the time you work your way through your first Flash tutorial, Shockwave may be considered standard, too. Animation is one area of Web design where advances come fast and furious.

☆ Summary

▶ The GIF and JPEG file formats both work well, albeit for different types of images. GIFs are well suited to line art, logos, and pictures of text. JPEGs are a better option for photographs and images that require a large color palette.

▶ Thumbnail previews conserve bandwidth and give visitors an opportunity to decide which images deserve to be downloaded in their entirety.

▶ Transparent GIFs are easy to create, although you must perform some image editing to work with an image from a photograph.

▶ Image maps add clickable regions to Web pages within button panels and other graphical navigation devices. You can create them with either special software utilities or just a Web browser (if you know the ISMAP trick).

▶ You can add simple animations to your Web pages by including animated GIF files, or you can opt for more sophisticated animations by working with streaming media technologies.

☆ Online References

LZW and GIF Explained
`http://www.msg.net/utility/whirlgif/lzw.html`

The GIF Controversy: A Software Developer's Perspective
`http://www.cloanto.com/users/mcb/19950127giflzw.html`

PNG (Portable Network Graphics)
`http://www.libpng.org/pub/png/`

MediaBuilder GIFWorks
`http://ruel.net/graphics/index.htm?`

Correct and Beautiful Transparent GIFs with Photoshop
`http://www.webdesignclinic.com/ezine/v1i2/trans/`

Animated GIFs from WebDeveloper.com
`http://webdeveloper.com/animations/`

Getting into Motion: A Guide for Adding Animation to Your Web Pages
`http://webdeveloper.com/design/design_getting_motion.html`

Constructing Animations (a Tutorial)
`http://member.aol.com/royalef/gifmake.htm`

GIF Animators
`http://animation.about.com/arts/animation/cs/gifanimators/`
`index.htm`

Streaming Media World
`http://streamingmediaworld.com`

☆ Review Questions

1. What is an adaptive color palette? Which image format supports it?

2. What sorts of images work well in the GIF format? Which ones work well in the JPEG format?

3. What is a progressive JPEG?

4. Why is a lossy file format the best choice for thumbnail previews?

5. What is a transparent GIF?

6. Explain how GIF photographs must be modified before you can make them transparent.

7. Which three attributes go into an `AREA` tag when you create an image map?

8. Suppose that a button is 30 pixels high and 50 pixels wide, and its lower-left corner is located at the coordinates (320, 100). What is the `COORDS` value for this button in an image map?

9. What is the simplest way to add animation to a Web page?

10. How does streaming media work?

☆ Hands-On Exercises

1. MediaBuilder GIFWorks (`http://ruel.net/graphics/index.htm?`) offers an online GIF editor that you can use to create transparent GIFs (among other things). Select an appropriate GIF file, and then visit GIFWorks to make a transparent version of your GIF. Test your file against a colored background to verify that it works correctly.

2. Go to Yahoo!'s home page (`http://www.yahoo.com/`) and examine the graphic at the top of the page. This image supports an image map with six `AREA` tags. Download this image to your local host by (1) positioning your mouse over the image, (2) holding down the right mouse button, and (3) selecting Save Image As in the resulting pop-up menu. (*Note*: Mac users can reach the same pop-up menu by holding their mouse button down for a second or two.) Save this image to your hard drive.

3. Using your local copy of the Yahoo! navigation bar (see Exercise 2), apply the `ISMAP` trick to map the six button regions. Point your browser at `http://www.yahoo.com/` and examine the status bar at the bottom of your Web browser as you roll your mouse over the navigation bar at the top of the page. Collect the six link destinations for this image map, and then

use them to complete an image map based on your local copy of the Yahoo! navigation bar. When you finish this exercise, you should have a working version of the Yahoo! navigation bar in a local file.

4. Visit the Poor Person's Image Mapper (`http://www.pangloss.com/seidel/ClrHlpr/imagemap.html`) and generate coordinates for the Yahoo! image map (see Exercise 2) using this facility. (*Note*: You will have to enter an online address for the image file at this facility.)

5. (*For Microsoft Word and/or Netscape users*) Even if you don't have an image editor or file converter, you may still be able to convert certain image files into a Web-friendly file format. For example, you can convert many image file formats to GIF files using Microsoft Word. Open an empty Word document and drag your image file into the document window. From the File menu, select Save As HTML. Word will create an `.htm` file as well as a GIF file in the same subdirectory. To see the name of the GIF file, view the source file for the `.htm` file. Similarly, you can convert any `.bmp` file to a JPEG file with Netscape's Composer (and many other HTML editors). Just open a Composer window and drag the `.bmp` file into the Composer window. Composer will then ask you where you want to save the JPEG image and which quality level option to apply. Try to convert some BMP, TIFF, or PICT files using Word, Composer, or another HTML editor. How do the new files compare to the old files with respect to file size?

CHAPTER SIX

TABLES

Tables are normally associated with numerical data and spreadsheets. An HTML table is far more versatile than a spreadsheet table, however. HTML tables are used to control Web page layouts for both text and graphics, separate a Web page into independent regions, and overlay graphical elements such as background colors and patterns. Web pages without tables have limited visual appeal and flexibility; tables take Web page construction up to the next level.

Chapter Objectives

☆ Examine the structure of HTML tables

☆ Explore the most important table attributes

☆ Learn how tables can be used to format text

☆ Learn how tables can be used to format graphics

☆ Explain some caveats and warnings associated with tables

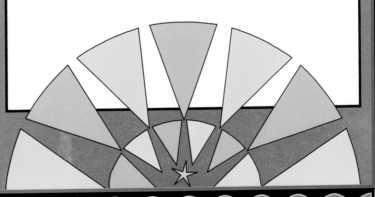

◎◎ Table Cells and Table Structure

The **table element** (which is created with the `<table></table>` tag-pair) has an internal structure based on *rows* and *columns*. In terms of tags, each HTML table requires a distinct **table row element** (created with the `<tr></tr>` tag-pair) for each row of the table. Each row, in turn, includes distinct **table data elements** (created with the `<td></td>` tag-pair) for every entry in that particular row. The simplest possible table is a table that has only one row and one data element.

> ☆**WARNING** Close All Table Tags
>
> If you forget to close off a table by including the `</table>` tag, Internet Explorer will display your table element despite the missing termination tag. Conversely, Netscape Navigator will refuse to display the entire table as well as the remainder of your HTML file. As a result, Web pages that look fine in Internet Explorer may be completely blank when viewed with Navigator. Similar discrepancies will occur if you omit any `</tr>` or `</td>` tags.

Each of the two tables shown in Figure 6.1 contains one table row, and within that row is one table data element (often called a **cell**). Table data elements can contain any HTML elements you like. This statement leads to a simple rule: If you can add it to a Web page, you can add it to a table cell.

Tables are especially well suited for organizing data collections and should be used whenever you need to display a chart. When used for a chart, table cells can hold two types of information: headers and data. A sequence of TH elements in the first row creates a header for each table column, and TD elements are used throughout the remaining rows for data entries. Figure 6.2 shows a course syllabus formatted for the Web using a table with many table rows and five table data elements per row.

```
<table bgcolor="blue">      <!-- first table -->
   <tr>
     <td>
        <font face="helvetica" size="6" color="white">
        This is the first table with a blue background.
        </font>
                                          </td>
                                          </tr>
   </table>


<table bgcolor="yellow">   <!-- second table -->
   <tr>
     <td>
        <font face="helvetica" size="6">
        This is the second table with a yellow background.
        </font>
                                          </td>
                                          </tr>
   </table>
```

Figure 6.1 Two Single-Cell Tables (*continues*)

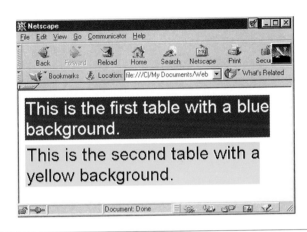

Figure 6.1 Two Single-Cell Tables

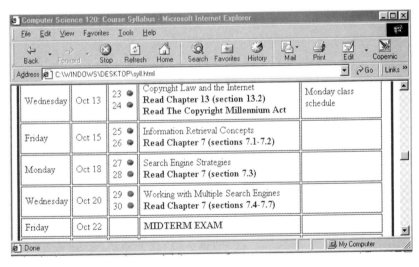

Figure 6.2 A Course Syllabus in a Table

Tables normally take up only as much space as is necessary to display the contents of their cells, while maintaining constant cell dimensions within each row and each column. All cells in a given row have the same height, and all cells in a given column have the same width. The Web browser handles the process of determining these height and width dimensions. All the Web page author has to do is fill each cell with visible elements.

Table Attributes

You can modify tables by assigning table attributes, table row attributes, and table data attributes. In Figure 6.3, a JPEG image has been inserted into a single-cell table with a BORDER attribute. This attribute's value specifies the pixel width of the border—in this case, the border is 5 pixels wide. Note that the frame fits the image perfectly because the table cell will be sized automatically to match the image.

```
<body bgcolor="#D8E4E8">
<!-- start outer table -->
<table width="100%" bgcolor="#D8E4E8">
   <tr>
      <td align="center">
      <!-- start inner table -->
      <table border="5">
         <tr>
            <td>
            <img src="face.jpg" width="432" height="331">
                               </td>
                               </tr>
      </table>
      <!-- end inner table -->
                               </td>
                               </tr>
</table>
<!-- end outer table -->
</body>
```

> This color was chosen to match the background color in the image.

> The 100% width attribute for the outer table along with the center alignment for the outer table's data element guarantees that the inner table will always be horizontally centered inside the browser window.

> The border for the inner table takes on the background color of the outer table.

Figure 6.3 A JPEG Image Inside a Centered Table with a Border

To center the framed image on the Web page, you embed the bordered frame inside a second frame. Note that the outer table shown in Figure 6.3 has no border and is not visible on the Web page, but it nevertheless contributes to the page display by controlling the placement of the inner table on the Web page. To control the absolute width of a table, you can use pixel attribute values (integers only) for the table's WIDTH attribute. In most instances, it is considered more desirable to specify a percentage attribute value, which forces the table to occupy a certain percentage of the available horizontal space. When the browser window is resized, the table is then proportionately resized according to its WIDTH percentage.

The outer table in Figure 6.3 was designed to occupy 100% of the available space. If that were the sole attribute of the outer table, you wouldn't see the effect of its width attribute. When we combine proportional table dimensions with the assignment align="center" inside the TD tag, however, then the cell contents of the TD element will always be centered in the browser window—no matter how the window is resized.

The outer table in Figure 6.3 also has a BGCOLOR attribute. This color was selected to match the background color of the framed image so as to achieve an embedded look. That is, the matching colors make the image appear to be part of the Web page, even as the 3-D table border gives it the appearance of a framed picture resting on top of the Web page.

◎◎ Tables and Text

Figure 6.4 shows how tables can be used to display blocks of text. In this case, the Web page lays single-celled tables of text on top of a background pattern. The textured background enhances the visual appeal of the page, and the tables preserve the readability of the text. This approach represents a good way to keep smaller text fonts legible without sacrificing interesting background patterns.

You can also use tables to produce two-column text displays to achieve a newsletter effect. In this case, it is important to keep the columns narrow so that they will be displayed correctly on smaller monitors. To create a two-column text table, just create a table with one row and two data elements in that row. Fill each data element with a column of text. For the best results, you should add the same amount of text to each cell. Unfortunately, you cannot make the text flow from one column to the next, so you must balance the columns manually.

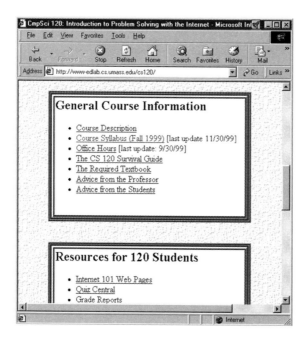

Figure 6.4 Single-Cell Tables on Top of a Background Pattern

Figure 6.5 demonstrates this idea by showing a table that contains one row and two columns. Extra white space has been placed between and around the columns by including a `CELLPADDING` attribute inside the `TABLE` tag with a value of 20 (pixels).

The `CELLPADDING` table attribute is a powerful tool for managing white space inside tables. The `CELLPADDING` values determine how much blank space should be inserted between adjacent cells and between each cell and the table border. In fact, tables offer many opportunities for white-space management. Suppose you want to run a border down the left side of your Web page (as shown in Figure 3.9, for example). In Chapter Three, you saw how a very wide image file can be tiled into a background pattern that produces a border running down the left side of the Web page. Unfortunately, if you enter text directly on top of a tiled background, the text will run into the border (see Figure 6.6). For this reason, you should keep borders and text separate from each other.

To keep text and other elements on your page away from a border, you can create a table with an empty column that runs down the left side of the page. Reserve this empty column for the border pattern, and then add a right-side column to hold all other visual elements on the Web page. In this way, you ensure that the two regions steer clear of each other (see Figure 6.7).

```
<table cellpadding="20">
    <tr>  <!-- first row -->
        <td>
        -- insert column one text here --
                                                </td>

        <td>
        -- insert column two text here --
                                                </td>
                                                </tr>
</table>
```

This creates a 20-pixel margin inside each table cell.

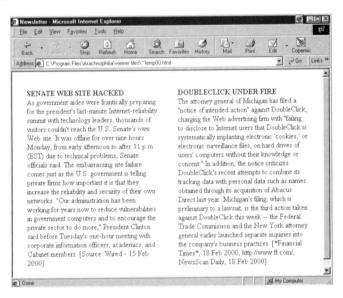

Figure 6.5 Text in a Two-Column Format Using Two Table Cells

Figure 6.6 Text Can Run into Web Page Borders

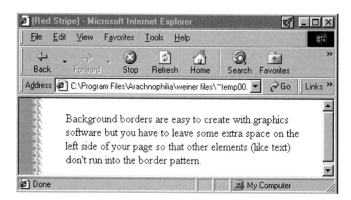

Figure 6.7 An Empty Table Column Keeps Text Separate from a Page Border

To include a solid bar that runs down the left side of your Web page, you don't even need a background graphic. For a solid bar, just add a table column with a fixed WIDTH attribute and a BGCOLOR attribute.

☆**TIP**   **Empty Table Cells for Empty Spaces**

When you want a table cell to act as a spacing device, you must insert a blank character ( ) into the cell so that it will be displayed properly. If you leave a table cell completely empty, it will not show up on your Web page, *even if you give the cell a nonzero WIDTH attribute.*

☆**WARNING** **Not All Browsers Display Tables**

Although tables can be very effective with text, think carefully before you put a lot of text into a multicolumn format. Some Web browsers do not support tables, which means that Web pages like those shown in Figures 6.2 and 6.5 may be difficult or impossible to read with certain Web browsers (most notably, the text-based browser Lynx and browsers designed for visually impaired people).

◎ Tables and Graphics

Clearly, tables are a very powerful device in designing Web page layouts. Table cells can hold text, graphics, or hyperlinks, and each cell can have its own background pattern or background color. In addition, you can modify the sizes of table cells so that different cells have different sizes. When a table's cells depart from uniformly spaced rows and columns, predictable boundaries based on a fixed number of rows and columns become less apparent, and your Web page can take on a more fluid look.

If all of your images are the same size, then a uniform table with a fixed number of rows and columns is all you need. On the other hand, if you plan to use different-sized images, you might require a table that has a different number of columns in each row or a different number of rows in each column. Figure 6.8

☆TIP   BORDER="1"

When you are experimenting with complicated table layouts (and especially if you are not very experienced with tables), set the table BORDER attribute equal to "1" so that you can see exactly where each cell lies. This assignment will save you a lot of time and frustration while you are learning.

shows an art gallery layout consisting of one table with two table rows, three TD elements in the first row (the three images bordering the top of the Web page) and one TD element in the second row (the image in the middle, at the bottom of the page). You create such irregular cell dimensions by using a table data ROWSPAN attribute. To see how to insert ROW-SPAN attributes, grab a pencil and a piece of paper so that you can sketch out a cell structure diagram.

```
<table>
  <tr>   <!-- first row   -->
    <td rowspan="2" align="center" >
      <img src="fox1thin.jpg" width="247" height="602" >
                                              </td>
    <td align="center" >
      <img src="wink.jpg" width="312" height="222" >
                                              </td>
    <td rowspan="2" align="center" >
      <img src="sila1thin.jpg" width="222" height="608" >
                                              </td>
                                              </tr>
  <tr>   <!-- second row   -->
    <td align="center" >
      <img src="sila2.jpg" width="267" height="334" >
                                              </td>
                                              </tr>
</table>
```

Figure 6.8 One Table with Two Table Rows and Four Table Data Elements

To create a table layout in which cells extend across multiple rows, begin by drawing a sketch of the final layout. Position rectangles next to each other, with each rectangle representing an image or a block of text needed for your page. Next, study your sketch to see how many rows are needed for the longest column and how many columns are needed for the longest row. The target layout in Figure 6.8 needs two rows for the second column, and three columns for the first row (it also needs three columns for the second row). Using these row and table counts, draw a second sketch consisting of a simple grid with uniform rows and columns. The grid for Figure 6.8, for example, should contain two rows and three columns. This grid constitutes the *cell structure* for the table layout.

Step 1: The Target Layout   **Step 2:** The Cell Structure

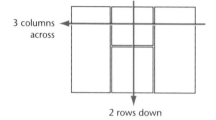

3 columns
across

2 rows down

Now compare the target layout with the cell structure and determine which cells should be joined and occupied by a single table data element. When a cell extends across two or more rows, draw an arrow across the locations in the cell structure that should be joined. All ROWSPAN extensions extend downward from the actual position of the table data element being extended. If you find it helpful, color the different rectangles in the target layout and then duplicate those colors in the cell structure diagram (see Figure 6.9). When you add your arrows to the cell structure diagram, make sure that all arrows spanning multiple rows point downward—never upward.

   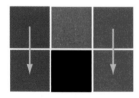

Figure 6.9 A Target Layout and Its Underlying Cell Structure

Once you have added the arrows to the cell structure diagram, you are ready to create a table element. The cell structure diagram shows how many rows go into the table, so add those elements first. The tricky part is determining the locations of the various data elements. When you have the cell structure diagram in front of you, however, this step is easy. You need to remember only two rules:

TD Rule 1: Each row receives a TD element whenever that row contains either (1) a cell with no arrow in it or (2) a cell with the beginning of an arrow in it (the end opposite to the arrow head).

TD Rule 2: Any TD tag corresponding to a cell that contains the beginning of a downward-pointing arrow receives a ROWSPAN attribute with a value equal to the length of the arrow (as measured by the number of rows traversed).

For our example in Figure 6.9, Rule 1 tells you to put three TD elements in the first row and one TD element in the second row. Rule 2 tells you to add rowspan="2" to the first and third TD tags in the first row. Once all of the tag-pairs are in place, you have completed the table structure. All that remains is to insert images or text into each of the TD elements as needed.

Whereas the ROWSPAN attribute extends table cells downward across multiple table rows, the COLSPAN attribute extends table cells to the right across multiple table columns. Figure 6.10 shows a Web page layout that uses both ROWSPAN and COLSPAN attributes.

```
<table>
   <tr>    <!-- first row -->
     <td rowspan="2">
       <img src="church1.jpg" alt="Ashby Town Green"
         align= "left" width="152" height="200">    </td>

     <td colspan="2">
       <h1 align="center"> <font face="helvetica">
         West on Route 119 </font></h1>            </td>
                                                   </tr>
   <tr>    <!-- second row -->
     <td>
       <img src="ma-trans.gif" alt="Map of rte 119"
         width="204" height="118" >                </td>
     <td>
       <font face="helvetica"><strong> Take a scenic
       drive to north central Massachusetts. It's only
       about an hour from Boston. (Click on the pictures
       to learn more.)
       </strong></font>                            </td>
                                                   </tr>
</table>
```

Figure 6.10 Tables Can Combine Graphics and Text *(continues)*

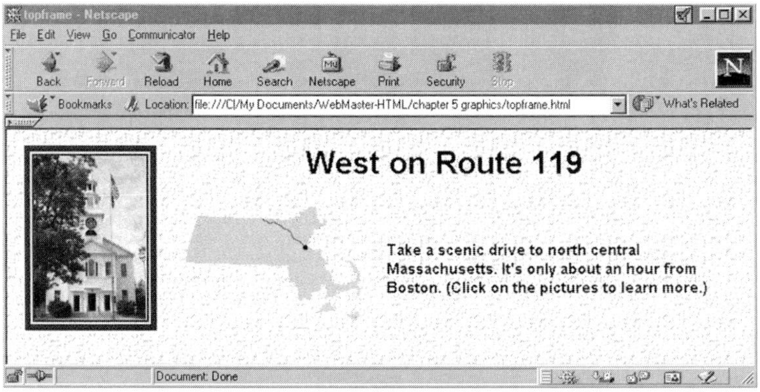

Figure 6.10 Tables Can Combine Graphics and Text

To create a Web page layout like the one shown in Figure 6.10, you start by piecing together the individual components in a sketch. Figure 6.11 shows the individual graphic and text components employed in Figure 6.10. The red rectangles reveal the underlying structure of the target layout.

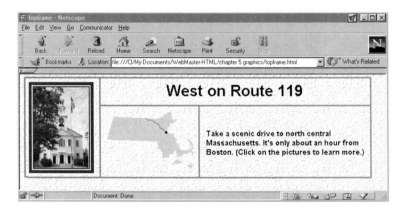

Figure 6.11 This Table Requires Both ROWSPAN and COLSPAN Attributes

Next, sketch the rectangles for the target layout on a piece of paper along with the underlying cell structure for your layout (see Figure 6.12). Place the picture of the target structure next to the cell structure diagram, and then add to the cell structure downward-pointing arrows for the regions that span two or more rows. Next, look for regions that extend across two or more columns. For each of those regions, add a horizontal arrow pointing to the right (never add a column-spanning arrow that points to the left).

 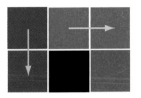

Figure 6.12 Another Target Layout and Underlying Cell Structure

With the cell structure diagram shown in Figure 6.12 in hand, you are now ready to craft the table needed for the Web page shown in Figure 6.10. You just need to add a third TD rule:

TD Rule 3: Any TD tag corresponding to a cell that contains the beginning of a rightward-pointing arrow receives a COLSPAN attribute with a value equal to the length of the arrow (as measured by the number of columns traversed).

Using Figure 6.12 and the three TD rules, try to generate a table structure for the Web page shown in Figure 6.10. Check your table code to see whether it matches the HTML code given in Figure 6.10. Your finished table should look just like the one in the book, except that your TD elements will be empty.

◎◎ Tables and Web Page Layouts

As we've seen, tables are powerful tools in the quest to create complicated Web page layouts. If you can imagine a layout, you can create a table to realize it. Figure 6.13 shows a Web page layout that could be broken down into 10 separate elements. Using ROWSPAN and COLSPAN attributes, you could produce this layout by creating a table containing six rows and four columns.

Each table and each table data element in a Web page layout can specify its own BGCOLOR or BACKGROUND attribute to create separate regions and demarcate clear divisions between the main elements on a Web page. In fact, each table data element operates like a tiny, separate Web page. You can set different FONT attributes and ALIGN attributes within each table cell, and all of the cells will coexist peacefully without any interference.

Sometimes a group of table cells should share the same attribute values. Happily, you don't have to set the attributes for each cell separately. Instead, you can add an ALIGN attribute to a table row element, and each cell in that row will then share the same alignment setting. Note that if you add an ALIGN attribute to the TABLE tag, all cells inside the table won't be aligned; rather, text will flow around the table, just as the ALIGN attribute in an IMG tag makes text flow alongside an IMG element.

Several other table attributes worth mastering—most notably, CELLPADDING and CELLSPACING. Earlier, you saw how CELLPADDING proved useful in formatting a two-column text layout. For a good explanation of the differences between CELLPADDING and CELLSPACING, see "The Not-So-Basic Table" in the list of recommended URLs at the end of this chapter.

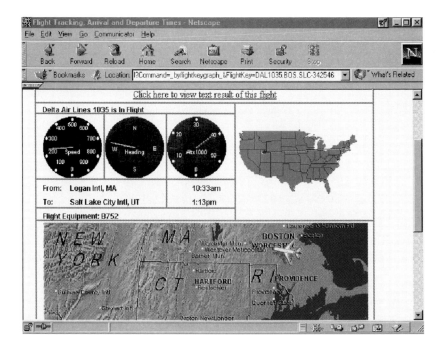

Figure 6.13 Tables Facilitate the Creation of Complicated Page Layouts

☆ **TIP   Many Is Better Than Few**

Whenever possible, break up large tables with many rows into a series of smaller tables (not nested). Your page will download more quickly and will be displayed incrementally, giving visitors something to ponder while the rest of the page is loading.

Now that you have witnessed some of the benefits that tables provide, a word of caution is in order. Tables inevitably slow down Web pages to some extent. As a rule, the more table elements on a Web page, the more slowly that page downloads. For this reason, you should not add any unnecessary table rows or table data elements. Avoid redundant or extraneous tag attributes as well. It's best to avoid nested tables unless they are essential, especially when the tables in question are complicated (Netscape Navigator sometimes just gives up when confronted with too many nested tables.) Finally, graphics-intensive tables can take a long time to download and render, so be careful not to add too many graphics to a single table.

☆ **TIP**   **GIF Snapshots of Tables**

If you have a complicated table layout that is relatively small and stable, consider replacing it with a GIF image. Display the table with your browser, take a screenshot of the display, crop the image, and convert it to a GIF file. If you are working with nested tables, the interior tables may be especially good candidates for conversion to GIFs. Just be careful to include a satisfactory ALT tag for those browsers that cannot display graphics. In many cases, a GIF image will download more rapidly than a nested table. If dynamic resizing is not a concern, compact table displays often work well as GIFs.

The W3C recommends that tables be reserved exclusively for tabular data, with Web page layouts being managed with Cascading Style Sheets instead (see Chapter Two for a discussion of CSS in the context of deprecated HTML elements). This guideline is good advice, for many reasons, in addition to the practical problems associated with tables. Although Web page layouts based on tables are appropriate for beginners and amateurs, if you intend to acquire the skills of a professional Web page designer, you should look beyond HTML and into CSS to discover more powerful approaches to creating Web page layouts.

Table 6.1 summarizes HTML attributes related to tables.

Table 6.1 Selected Table-Related Attributes

HTML Element	Attributes	Attribute Values	What the Attribute Does
`<table>` `</table>`	`align=`	`left`, `right`	Justifies the table against one side of the page with text flowing down alongside it (*Note:* This attribute does *not* set the alignment for any cells within the table.)
	`bgcolor=`	[a color name or hexadecimal color code]	Sets the background color for all cells of the table (can be overridden by `TD BGCOLOR`)
	`border=`	n (an integer)	Sets the width in pixels of the beveled (3-D) border drawn around the entire table (the default value is 0); a non-0 border shows cell boundaries
	`cellpadding=`	n (an integer)	Sets the width in pixels of a margin inserted inside the boundaries for each cell (the default value is 2)
	`cellspacing=`	n (an integer)	Sets the width in pixels of the boundary separating adjacent cells (the default value is 2)

(continues)

Table 6.1 Selected Table-Related Attributes *(continued)*

HTML Element	Attributes	Attribute Values	What the Attribute Does
	summary=	[a quoted string]	Summarizes the table for nonvisual browsers
	width=	n (an integer), or n%	An integer value sets the width of the table in pixels; a percentage value sets the width as a percentage of the width of the browser window
`<td></td>` (table data) `<th></th>` (table headers)	align=	left, center, right	Sets the horizontal alignment for one cell (the default value is left)
	bgcolor=	[a color name or hexadecimal color code]	Sets the background color for one cell
	colspan=	n (an integer)	Allows the cell to span n table columns
	nowrap	[takes no value]	Keeps all text inside the cell on a single line, unless explicitly broken with BR or P tags
	rowspan=	n (an integer)	Allows the cell to span n table rows
	valign=	top, middle, bottom, baseline	Sets the vertical alignment for one cell (the default value is middle)
	width=	n (an integer)	An integer value sets the width of the cell in pixels
`<tr></tr>` (table row)	align=	left, center, right	Sets the alignment attribute for each cell in one row (can be overridden by TD ALIGN)
	nowrap	[takes no value]	Disables line wrapping for all cells in the row
	valign=	top, middle, bottom, baseline	Sets the vertical alignment for all cells in the row (the default value is middle)

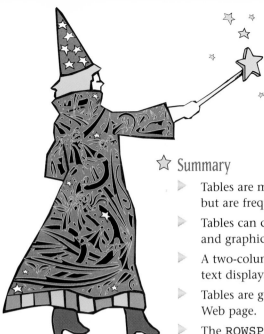

☆ Summary

▷ Tables are most appropriate for displays of tabular data, but are frequently used for Web page layouts as well.

▷ Tables can contain text, graphics, combinations of text and graphics, and other tables.

▷ A two-column table can be used to format a two-column text display.

▷ Tables are generally useful for managing white space on a Web page.

▷ The ROWSPAN and COLSPAN attributes can be used to create irregular tables.

▷ The W3C does not support the use of HTML tables for Web page layouts, but rather suggests that Cascading Style Sheets be used for this purpose instead.

☆ Online References

Page Layout, Margins, Indenting, and Columns (from Hacks to Style Sheets)
`http://wdvl.com/Authoring/Design/Layout/index.html`

Using Tables for Web Site Layout (Contains a Discussion of Table Width and Monitor Resolution)
`http://www.webdevelopersjournal.com/diary/10_24.html`

The Not-So-Basic Table (a Good Explanation of CELLPADDING versus CELLSPACING)
`http://hotwired.lycos.com/webmonkey/96/48/index2a.html?tw=authoring`

Tables: W3C Recommendation (Learn about More Attributes)
`http://www.w3.org/TR/REC-html40/struct/tables.html`

Create Tables That Are Transformed Gracefully (Problems with Using Tables as Layout Devices)
`http://www.w3.org/TR/WAI-WEBCONTENT/#gl-table-markup`

Tables on Non-table Browsers (Tabular Tables for Lynx and Other Browsers That Do Not Support Tables)
`http://ppewww.ph.gla.ac.uk/~flavell/www/tablejob.html`

☆ Review Questions

1. Explain how `<tr>` and `<td>` tags work together inside table elements. Which one goes inside the other?

2. What will happen if you forget to close a table with the `</table>` tag?

3. Show how a table can be used to divide a Web page into two halves, split down the middle, with two different background colors and separate columns of text inside each half. Which attributes and attribute values would you use to ensure that a 20-pixel space always appeared between the two columns of text? Write the HTML code for the table that fulfills these criteria.

4. Show how a `TD` element can be used to create a 50-pixel margin so that nothing on the Web page interferes with a background pattern that runs down the left side of the page. Write the HTML code for the table that fulfills these criteria.

5. Show how a table can be used to create a 10-pixel black border that runs down the entire left side of a Web page. Write the HTML code for the table that fulfills these criteria.

6. Show how a table can be used to create two black borders, each 10 pixels wide, running down both the left and right sides of a Web page. Write the HTML code for the table that fulfills these criteria.

7. Show how a table can be used to horizontally position a GIF image in the center of a Web page, no matter how the browser window is resized. The image should rest directly on the page without any borders or frames surrounding it. Write the HTML code for the table that fulfills these criteria.

8. Explain what the `ALIGN` attribute does inside a `TD` tag. What does it do inside a `TR` tag? Inside a `TABLE` tag?

9. Suppose you place some red text inside one table cell but forget to close off the `FONT` element in that cell. Will the text in the next cell appear in red? If you are not sure of the answer to this question, conduct an experiment with a test table. Can you explain your results?

10. Describe an alternative to nested tables that may be preferable under certain circumstances. When would this alternative be a good idea, and why?

☆ Hands-On Exercises

1. Figure 3.1 was created with an HTML table. Re-create the image in Figure 3.1 by writing an `.html` file. Make your table fill up the entire width of the browser window, no matter how the window is resized.

2. Create a three-column text display similar to the two-column display shown in Figure 6.5. Experiment with different values for the `CELLPADDING` attribute. What is a good `CELLPADDING` value for your text display? Give your table a `BGCOLOR` attribute, and experiment by replacing the `CELLPADDING` attribute with a `CELLSPACING` attribute. Which attribute looks better when the text columns have their own `BGCOLOR`? Explain your reasoning.

3. In Chapter 5, you learned how to make image maps. Armed with a table and some image files, you can make a "pseudo-image map" that is indistinguishable from the real thing. Try it yourself with the following table:

```
<table cellpadding="5" cellspacing="0" border="0">
<tr>
  <td bgcolor="orange"><b> Home          </td>
  <td bgcolor="aqua"><b> Site Map       </td>
  <td bgcolor="yellow"><b> Contact Us    </td>
                                          </tr>
</table>
```

Display this table with a Web browser and then take a screen shot of the browser window. To take a simple screen shot, press [Alt] + [Prt Sc] on a Windows computer or [⌘] + [Shift] + [3] on a Macintosh computer. Load the resulting screen shot into a graphics utility, and then crop the image. Save a separate image of each of the three rectangles, being careful to make all of the rectangles the same height. Reassemble the images in a table, turning each image into a link label for some link destination. (*Note*: Windows users can download a freeware utility called Splitz! that breaks up images as directed and automatically reassembles them in a table.) Your table should have the CELLPADDING, CELLSPACING, and BORDER attributes all set to 0. To eliminate the blue border around each image, add a BORDER=0 attribute to each IMG as well.

A Challenge Problem: If your table includes a gap between adjacent table cells, modify it to eliminate those spaces.

4. Study the following code and predict how it will display the table. Draw a picture of the table you expect this code to generate. Next, type the code into an .html file and display it in your Web browser. Is the display what you expected? If not, modify the HTML code until it generates the table that you drew.

```
<table border="1" cellpadding="0" CELLSPACING="10">
  <tr align="center">
    <td width="25%" bgcolor="red" rowspan="1">
                                     </td>
    <td width="50%" bgcolor="yellow">
                        Hello Sunshine!   </td>
    <td width="25%" bgcolor="orange">    </td>
                                          </tr>
  <tr>
    <td colspan="1" bgcolor="black">     </td>
                                          </tr>
</table>
```

5. Draw a cell structure diagram for the Web depicted in Figure 6.13. Code an HTML table based on your cell structure diagram, filling in each cell with some text. Set the BORDER attribute to 1 so that you can see the cell boundaries, and then display your table in a Web browser. Compare your table layout with the layout in Figure 6.13 and make any modifications needed if they do not match (exact cell sizing does not matter here—you just want to match the cell structure).

CHAPTER SEVEN

FRAMES

Web sites containing more than a few Web pages require thoughtful organization. Although first-time visitors should be able to navigate large Web sites quickly and effortlessly, this will not happen without careful planning on the part of the site designer. Frames are an effective tool for organizing large Web sites and making them easy to navigate. Frames are especially appropriate for sites with Web pages that are frequently modified or updated, and they impose a useful structure on Web sites that are maintained by more than one person. Nevertheless, frames do have some disadvantages that you should consider before adopting a frames-based approach to your entire Web site.

Chapter Objectives

☆ Show how to construct frames-based displays

☆ Explain how frames can be used to facilitate Web site navigation

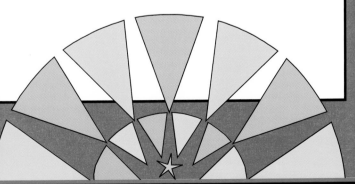

☆ Show how to make an easy-to-browse art or photo gallery with frames

☆ Explore the controversial practice of deep linking

◎◎ Anatomy of a Frame

HTML **frames** partition a browser window into predefined regions so that different HTML files can be displayed inside each region. Thus a frames-based display consists of one Web page that displays multiple Web pages. Although each frame remains an independent entity, frames become even more interesting when they interact with one another. For example, Web site designers often insert hyperlinks in one frame that alter the content inside a different frame.

You have probably seen frames in action at search engine sites, Web portal sites, and other large commercial sites where frames are frequently used as navigational aids. Some sites rely on a horizontal frame, which runs along the top of each Web page and contains links to important regions of the site. Other sites include a vertical frame that runs along the left (sometimes right) side of each Web page for the same purpose. Still other sites use both types of frames.

To create a frame, you insert a FRAMESET element immediately after the end of the HEAD element on your Web page. Whenever you include a FRAMESET element in an HTML file, you do not need a BODY element; the FRAMESET replaces the BODY. The FRAMESET element divides the browser window into separate frame regions. The visible content for those regions doesn't come from the FRAMESET element itself, however. To provide the content, you must fill the FRAMESET with HTML files. A Web page with a FRAMESET element does not contain any visible content of its own; rather, it can display only content found in other HTML files.

The FRAMESET element divides the browser window into separate frames using a COLS attribute, a ROWS attribute, or both. Each COLS and ROWS attribute takes as its value a list of percentage values separated by commas. A page with a single COLS attribute will be divided into a specified number of vertical columns. A page with a single ROWS attribute will be divided into horizontal rows. A page with both COLS and ROWS attributes will be divided into rectangular subsections. For example, the code

```
<frameset cols="35%, 65%" rows="60%, 40%">
```

divides the Web page into four frames (see Figure 7.1). The vertical divider appears 35% of the way in from the left side of the window, and the horizontal divider is placed 60% of the way down from the top. Although you can divide the page into as many rows and columns as you like, most layouts require only two rows (for a horizontal navigation bar) or two columns (for a vertical navigation panel). You can specify a frame region in two ways: as a percentage of the available space or in terms of some fixed number of pixels. A fixed pixel size is typically employed for navigation bars and panels. To achieve more complicated layouts, you can nest frames.

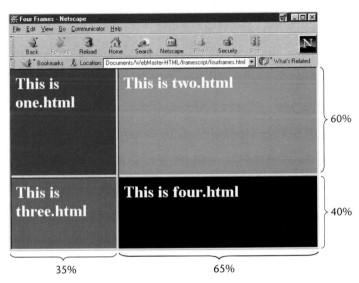

Figure 7.1 A Web Page Divided into Four Frames

To fill your frames with visible content, you first insert some **FRAME** elements inside the **FRAMESET** element and then specify a **SRC** attribute for each frame. For example, the following code produces the Web page shown in Figure 7.1:

```
<html>
<head>
<title>four frames</title>
</head>
<frameset cols="35%, 65%" rows="60%, 40%">

<frame name="upperleft" src="one.html">
<frame name="upperright" src="two.html">

<frame name="lowerleft" src="three.html">
<frame name="lowerright" src="four.html">

</frameset>
</html>
```

Top Row

Bottom Row

☆ **WARNING Close Off Your FRAMESET**

Use of the **FRAMESET** element requires that you include the tag-pair `<frameset></frameset>`. If you forget to close the **FRAMESET** element, some browsers will punish you with a blank page display.

Note that the frames are filled in from the top row to the bottom row, moving across the columns from left to right.

Each frame tag supports a number of attributes that provide for customized frame displays. For example, a default frame includes a vertical scroll bar for pages that will not fit in the available space. To omit the scroll bar, you can override this default with the frame attribute `scrolling="no"`.

☆**WARNING** **Frames without Scroll Bars**

Some people like to remove the scroll bar from frames whenever possible to maintain a cleaner, more streamlined look. If you are tempted to eliminate the default scroll bar, make sure that you have thoroughly tested your page under a variety of browsers, operating systems, and monitor resolution settings to verify that the contents of the frame will be fully visible for all members of your audience. There is nothing worse than a frame without a scroll bar that doesn't display its contents completely. *It is easy to create a frame that is displayed appropriately on a high-resolution monitor but fails miserably on low-resolution (640 × 480) displays.* Also note that the default value inserts a scroll bar only when it is needed, which is normally what you want.

A popular frame layout (shown in Figure 7.2) consists of three frames: (1) a title bar, (2) a button panel for site navigation, and (3) a content frame that responds to the button panel. Two nested FRAMESET elements are needed to achieve this three-frame layout.

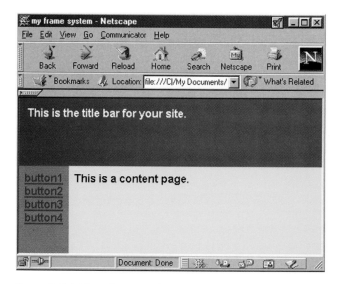

Figure 7.2 A Three-Frame Web Site Layout

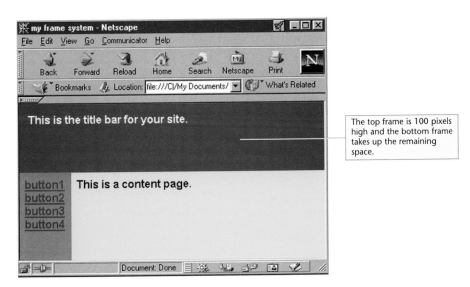

The top frame is 100 pixels high and the bottom frame takes up the remaining space.

Figure 7.3 The Top-Level FRAMESET Layout

The first frameset divides the display into a top half and a bottom half. That is, one FRAMESET divides the display into a frame for the title bar at the top of the page, and a second FRAMESET creates the remainder of the page (see Figure 7.3). The HTML code for the top-level FRAMESET follows:

```
<html>
<head><title> my frame system </title>
</head>
<frameset rows="100,*" frameborder="0"
         framespacing="0" border="0">
    <frame name="top" src="top.html" scrolling="no">
    <frame name="bottom" src="bottom.html">
</frameset>
</html>
```

☆**TIP   Frames and Browsers Display Updates**

When you are designing frames, you may discover that your browser's Reload or Refresh button no longer seems to work. Browsers must labor more intensely to load a frames-based Web page because they may be dealing with multiple HTML files. To ensure the your browser is providing the most recent version of your frames, hold down the Shift key when you hit Reload or Refresh.

Notice how the top frame is specified by pixels instead of a percentage value. In this case, we have assigned a vertical space of 100 pixels to the top frame. The asterisk tells the browser to fill in the rest of the display with any remaining space in the current browser window. Any resizing of the browser window will then affect how much of the bottom frame is visible; the top frame stays fixed at 100 pixels. Also, note the SRC attributes for the top and bottom frames. The file top.html contains visible content (see Figure 7.3). Conversely, the file bottom.html does not contain any visible content; it holds a second FRAMESET. Figure 7.4 shows the appearance of bottom.html when it is displayed by itself.

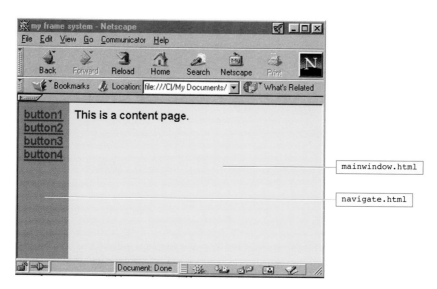

Figure 7.4 The Interior-Level FRAMESET Layout

All of the content in Figure 7.4 comes from the files navigate.html and mainwindow.html, even though we are looking at bottom.html. The actual code for bottom.html follows:

```
<html>
<head><title> my frame system </title></head>
<frameset cols="80, *" frameborder="0" framespacing="0"
        border="0" >
    <frame name="left" src="navigate.html"
        scrolling="no">
    <frame name="main" src="mainwindow.html">
</frameset>
</html>
```

> The left frame is 80 pixels wide and the right frame takes up any remaining space.

When creating FRAME elements, you should always include a NAME attribute for each frame. This practice will help you keep your frames straight—and you will definitely need names if you want to set up hyperlinks in one frame that can alter the content in a different frame. The next section provides an example of this type of linking.

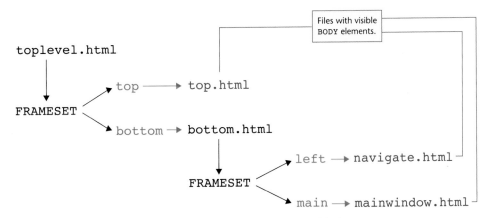

Figure 7.5 A Nested FRAMESET Layout for a Three-Frame Display

Figure 7.5 shows the **FRAMESET** structure for our three-frame display layout. Large Web sites often employ a similar layout. A navigation panel on the left contains links, and the main frame displays the content associated with those links. Next, we will look more closely at the use of frames for Web site navigation.

Frames-Based Navigation Menus

When you build a large Web site that includes many pages, you need to think carefully about navigational features. Visitors who are not familiar with your site will need signs and guideposts to find their way around. Navigation bars and panels are useful tools for this purpose for large Web sites, and you'll make life easier on your visitors if you display the *same* navigational options on all of your Web pages. In effect, you want one part of each Web page to remain consistent across your entire site. You can accomplish this goal by presenting the same navigational map on each page. To ensure this consistency, you could insert copies of the same table or image map on each Web page. That would be tedious for you, however, and, more importantly, would represent a nonoptimal use of bandwidth. Frames offer a much better solution.

Figure 7.6 shows a page display based on three frames. Two frames remain constant throughout the site: a title bar and a navigation menu. The remaining frame changes its display when the user clicks particular buttons in the navigation menu. This variable frame comprises the content frame.

The layout shown in Figure 7.6 is identical to the three-frame layout depicted in Figure 7.2. The top and left frames use the same background pattern, yielding a coherent "feel" for the fixed frame displays. Only the content frame (the main frame in Figure 7.5) changes as users navigate the site.

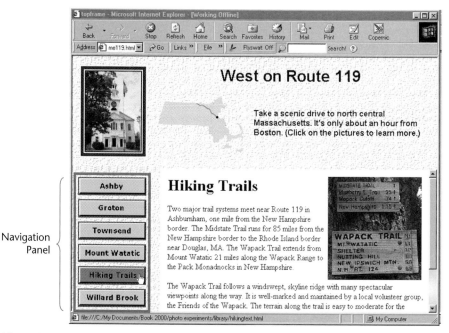

Figure 7.6 A Navigation Panel in a Frames-Based Display

☆**TIP** **Seamless Frames**

To have a background color or graphic mesh seamlessly across frames, remove the borders between your frames by setting the `FRAMESET` attributes as follows: `frameborder="0"` and `border="0"`.

☆**TIP** **Tell-Tale Blue Borders**

If you use an `IMG` element for a link label, a blue border will surround the image. To remove those borders, set the `IMG` attribute as follows: `border=0`.

You can create clickable navigation menus in several ways. For example, you can make a simple navigation menu from a list of text-based hyperlinks. To add a little color, place each link inside a table cell and then change the background color for each cell. If you add a lot of cell spacing to your table, the cells will look like buttons. When using such a table for hyperlinks, you can eliminate the blue underlining normally associated with text-based hyperlinks by replacing your text links with clickable image files. Just use the entire `IMG` element as your link label inside each table cell (see Exercise 3 in Chapter Six). Alternatively, you can create navigation bars or panels by using **image maps** (see Chapter Five).

Figure 7.7 shows a horizontal navigation bar based on a simple table display.

A link in one frame normally loads the link destination file into the same frame, unless you direct it to a different frame. When your Web page includes a frame for navigational purposes, the navigational frame should not be replaced when the user clicks a link in that frame. Instead, the requested page should be sent to a content frame. You can easily accomplish this goal by placing a `TARGET` attribute inside the A tag. To see how, let's look at an example based on the display in Figure 7.6 as well as the frame and filenames described in Figure 7.5.

Figure 7.7 A Navigation Bar Based on an HTML Table

Suppose you want to create a link inside the left frame (`navigate.html`) that will bring up a page about hiking trails in the main frame (the content frame). You could insert the following anchor element and attributes inside `navigate.html`:

> This code opens the file named `hiking.html` inside the frame named `main`.

```
<a href="hiking.html" target="main">hiking trails</a>
```

When the user clicks the link, the left frame will remain unchanged, while the file `hiking.html` will be loaded into the main frame. You can refer to any frame by its name when you specify the value for a `TARGET` attribute, no matter what the structure of your frame system.

Frames-Based Art Galleries

One type of frames-based navigation system is especially useful when you are working with online art or photograph galleries. Figure 7.8 shows a layout for photograph gallery that makes it easy to display images on demand in the content window.

Figure 7.8 A Photo Gallery Using Frames

The page in Figure 7.8 uses thumbnail previews (described in Chapter Five) in its navigation panel. Each thumbnail preview occupies a table cell and operates as a clickable link leading to its original counterpart. Of course, you don't have to use thumbnail previews for the navigation panel; you could choose text labels instead. Text labels would work well for an album of historic places or a family photo album, whereas a collection of abstract art would be better served by thumbnail previews. If necessary, you could always combine text captions with thumbnail previews to get the best of both worlds in the navigational frame.

◎◎ Deep Linking and Other Problems with Frames

When working with frames, you have an opportunity to engage in a highly controversial practice—one that has generated more than a few lawsuits. Frames that are used to help people navigate their way through a single site do not raise any concerns. But no one can stop you from adding a navigational button that transfers the user out of your site and into someone else's Web site. Breaking out of the frame when linking to an external site is no different than following an absolute link to another Web site. The problem arises when the link destination stays inside the frame display. In that case, someone else's Web page is displayed in a context that makes it appear to be part of your Web site. If your site "borrows" the target content from a commercial site, the display of that content outside its original context could harm advertisers' ability to garner revenues.

A **deep link** results in a display that pulls content out of its original and intended context; the practice of adding such links to a Web site is called **deep linking**. Because some companies have sued Web page authors over deep linking, it is important to understand the issues involved. One line of reasoning claims that any link to a page in a Web site—other than a link to that site's home page—constitutes a deep link. If all links meeting that definition were prohibited, the vast majority of Web page authors would have to revise or eliminate many of their links.

Fortunately, a U.S. District Court has ruled that hyperlinks pointing to pages other than home pages are acceptable, as long as they do not involve deception or misrepresentation. In the latter case, frames can become perilous. For example,

☆ **WARNING** **If You Use Frames, Never Frame a Deep Link**

Whenever a Web page inside a frame contains an absolute URL, you run the risk of appearing to appropriate someone else's content for your own site. As a rule, you should avoid framing a deep link. You can accomplish this goal in two ways: by inserting TARGET attributes into all of your absolute links and by using a TARGET value that is not part of your frame system. That approach will break the link out of your frames, thereby making it clear to anyone who follows the link that the user has left your Web site.

Make sure that you use the same TARGET value each time you break out of your frames. It's bad enough to open one new browser window when the user clicks on a link (some people do not like it when new windows pop up on their computers); if your site starts opening new windows willy-nilly, however, your design becomes rude and inexcusable. Each time you open a new window, the user must eventually close it. In such cases, your Web site visitors will likely leave your site grumbling and cursing—and vowing never to return.

suppose a link alters the context in which content is viewed such that the content appears to belong to a site other than its original site. That type of deep linking is not defensible in court.

Never display someone else's Web page inside your own frame. Unfortunately, it is easy to do—you just include a hyperlink to an external URL on a Web page that is displayed inside a frame. When someone clicks on the link inside the frame, then the destination page (the external Web page) will be loaded into the same frame, making it look like it's just another page at your site (see Figure 7.9).

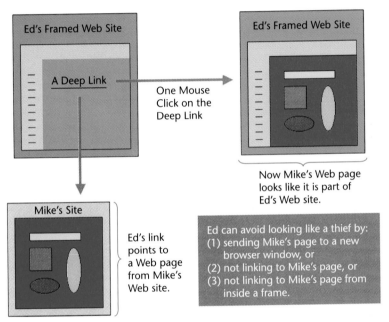

Figure 7.9 Deep Links Inside Frames Have Led to Lawsuits

☆**TIP**   **Keep Your Own Web Pages Free from Other People's Frames**

To ensure that none of your Web pages show up inside someone else's frame, you can block frames from loading your pages by making a preemptive strike against would-be "borrowers" in the form of a JavaScript directive. Insert the following line inside the BODY tag of each page you want to protect:

```
<body
onLoad="if(parent.frames.length!=0)top.location='MYpage.html';">
```

The file MYpage.html should be one of your own Web pages. If anyone tries to display that page inside his or her own frame, MYpage.html will then be displayed outside the frame in a new browser window, making it clear that your page is part of a different Web site. You probably want to insert the name of the page being loaded, so that viewers can still see the page that they originally requested (it's not their fault that your page was almost hijacked by a deep link inside a frame).

The only way to make sure that these external pages will not show up in your frames is to create hyperlinks that open all external URLs in a new browser window. Although you can readily accomplish this task, it must be done consistently across your entire Web site. For each absolute URL signifying an external Web page, insert a **TARGET** attribute inside the anchor:

```
<a href="www.yahoo.com" target="popup">
```

The value assigned to the **TARGET** attribute is not important, but you should use the same name for all external links. That way, each page will be sent to the same browser window. Otherwise, a new browser window will open each time someone clicks on one of these hyperlinks—a thoroughly impolite way to break out of the frame. Even opening one new browser window will annoy some users, because that window won't have a Back button that goes back any further than its creation.

If the prospect of deep linking infractions is not enough to make you reconsider constructing a frames-based site, some additional reasons exist to think twice about using frames. First and foremost, some browsers do not support frames. To ensure that everyone can see your site, you must offer two site options: one for people who can view frames, and one for people who can't. Second, even users who can see frames with their browsers may not know how to break out of the frame to print or bookmark a Web page inside a frame. Third, search engines have trouble indexing Web pages that are located inside frames. And there's more.

☆ **SHORTCUT**   **Alternative Web Pages for Browsers That Don't Support Frames**

You can embed alternative Web pages in the same `.html` files that contain FRAMESET elements so as to accommodate browsers that don't support frames. Just add the tag-pair `<noframes></noframes>` at the end of the FRAMESET element, and place your alternative page inside the NOFRAMES element.

Consider the problem faced by other Web page authors who want to link to one of your pages. Linking to anything other than your home page is not possible. That is, referencing a specific Web page that normally appears only inside a content frame is very problematic. First, the other Web page authors must track down the URL for the page independent of your frame system (something most beginners cannot do). Then, if they manage to find the original URL, those authors will link to that page outside its intended frame. If you don't mind people seeing your content outside of your frames, that approach is acceptable. Some Web page authors design their pages with the expectation that the pages will always be viewed in the context of a certain frame, however. Indeed, it's very difficult to design a page that works well both inside and outside of a frame.

Any link to a Web page that is normally viewed inside a frame will necessarily point to that page outside its frame (no URLs exist for pages embedded inside

☆TIP   How to Break a Page Out of Its Frame

To print or bookmark a Web page inside a frame, you must break the page out of the frame. Similarly, to obtain the URL for a page being displayed inside a frame, you cannot simply grab the URL in your browser's location window. It points to the top-level frame as it was initially displayed— that is, before you started changing the display in the content frame. Instead, you must break out of the frame.

To do so, position the mouse over the frame containing the desired content, and click the right mouse button (Mac users should hold the mouse button down for a second or two). In the pop-up menu that appears, select "New Window with this Frame" or "Open Frame in New Window." The Web page will then appear in a new browser window. Within that window you can bookmark the page, print the page, or check the location window and find the desired URL.

frames), thereby pulling it out of the context in which the original author intended it to be viewed. The link may not add an unintended context (unless the linking author frames it inside his or her own frame), but it does take context away.

Clearly, placing pages inside frames encourages deep linking. Linking to a page inside a frame is impossible without a deep link.

☆TIP   Moving In and Out of Frames

If you like the ideas of using frames for some portion of your Web site but don't want to frame your entire site, you can structure your site so that only selected pages are framed. Pages that contain only relative links (links to your own pages) avoid deep linking problems, and some portion of your site may be fully self-contained in that sense. To enter a frameset, just link to a page containing a FRAMESET element. To leave the framed pages *without opening a new browser window*, add an exit link with the attribute target="_top". That link will then break you out of your own frameset.

Although it's not necessary to always avoid all frames, you should be aware of the controversy surrounding their application. Use frames only when their advantages outweigh the disadvantages. For example, frames allow site designers to separate the development of navigational devices from content development, allowing work to progress in each direction independently. This division of labor can prove advantageous for constructing large sites, for which a group of Web page authors must coordinate their efforts without stumbling over one another. Moreover, frames can lead to convenient layouts and intuitive navigation.

Perhaps the deep linking issues don't really concern you. Lawsuits in this area have typically been initiated by commercial concerns, when the practice was thought to shrink potential revenues because pages with advertisements were bypassed by too many readers. If you have no such concerns, and the other drawbacks do not outweigh the advantages of using frames, you might reasonably decide to include frames in your Web site. Just watch out for any deep links that don't belong inside your frames.

Table 7.1 describes some frames-related HTML attributes.

Table 7.1 Selected Frames-Related Attributes

Tags	Attributes	Attribute Values	What It Does
`<frame>`	`border=`	"N" (an integer)	Sets the width of the space around the frame in pixels. The default value is 5 pixels.
	`bordercolor=`	One of the 16 color names or a hexadecimal color code	Sets the color for one frame (in some cases, it will set the border for a whole row or column).
	`frameborder=`	"1" or "0"	Makes the borders around the frames sculpted (1) or not sculpted (0).
	`name=`	A string name	Used to reference this frame from a TARGET attribute.
	`noresize`	[no value needed]	Prevents visitors from resizing the frame via drag-and-drop. The default allows resizing.
	`marginwidth=`	"N" (an integer)	Sets the distance (in pixels) between the left and right boundaries of a frame and its contents.
	`marginheight=`	"N" (an integer)	Sets the distance (in pixels) between the top and bottom boundaries of a frame and its contents.
	`scrolling=`	"YES", "NO", "AUTO"	Shows a scroll bar all the time (YES), never (NO), or only when needed (AUTO). The default is AUTO.
	`src=`	A filename (relative or absolute)	Inserts the specified file into the frame.
	`target=`	A string name signifying a frame (as set by the NAME attribute) or a browser window	Sends the SRC file to the named location.

Table 7.1 Selected Frames-Related Attributes (continued)

Tags	Attributes	Attribute Values	What It Does
`<frameset>` `</frameset>`	`border=`	"N" (an integer)	Sets the width of the space between the frames in pixels. The default value is 5 pixels.
	`bordercolor=`	One of the 16 color names-, or a hexadecimal color code	Sets the colors for all frame borders in a frameset.
	`cols=`	"N" (an integer), "N%"(percentage), "*", or "N*"	Sets the width of the column in pixels, as a percentage of the available space, or, in the case of an asterisk (*), whatever is left over from the other frames. N* divides the space among frames proportionally.
	`frameborder=`	"1" or "0"	Makes the borders around the frames sculpted (1) or not sculpted (0).
	`rows=`	"N" (an integer), "N%"(percentage), "*", or "N*"	Sets the height of the row in pixels, as a percentage of the available space, or whatever is left over from the other frames. N* divides the space among frames proportionally.
`<noframes>` `</noframes>`			For Web pages with frames, insert this element just before the closing `</frameset>` tag and insert the alternative content for browsers that don't support frames inside the NOFRAMES element.

☆ Summary

> A frames-based Web page can display the contents of multiple Web pages simultaneously, with each Web page appearing in its own frame. Links in one frame can change the Web page being displayed in a different frame.

> Frames can separate the navigational aspects of a Web site from its content. This division is helpful for the user, who can navigate the site more easily, and beneficial for the site designer, who can manage the site more easily.

> You can use table-based button panels, thumbnail sketches, and image maps inside a navigational frame to control the Web page that is displayed inside a content frame.

> Frames are associated with some serious problems. Not all browsers support frames. Web page authors cannot link to pages inside frames without pulling a page out of its intended context. Search engines have trouble indexing frames-based sites. Deep linking inside frames has prompted lawsuits from aggrieved Web site owners, and no solution to the deep linking problem has emerged as yet.

☆ Online References

Mikodocs Guide to HTML: Frames
`http://www.idocs.com/tags/frames/frames.html`

Frames Are a Picnic
`http://www.hotwired.com/webmonkey/html/96/31/index3a.html`

Fun with Frames
`http://www.builder.com/Authoring/Frames/`

HTML 4.0: Frames
`http://htmlgoodies.earthweb.com/tutors/html4_frames.html`

Using Inline Frames
`http://www.pageresource.com/html/iframe.htm`

Judge Rules on Deep Linking
`http://dgl.com/itinfo/2000/it000330.html`

Thinking About Linking
`http://www.llrx.com/features/weblink1.htm`

Deep Linking: Its Future on the Web
`http://www.internet-law-firm.com/articles/`
`Deep%20linking%20Its%20future%20on%20the%20Web.htm`

☆ Review Questions

1. Which two attributes determine how many frames appear within one FRAMESET? Describe three types of attribute values that can determine the size of each frame.

2. Which Web page element can be replaced by a FRAMESET element?

3. When you insert FRAME elements inside a FRAMESET element, how do you know which ROWS and COLS dimensions apply to which frame?

4. How do you control whether a frame includes a scroll bar?

5. How do you create a Web page layout with three frames?

6. Which attribute do you use to send a link destination into a different frame? In which HTML tag does this attribute go? Which other attribute in which other HTML tag is needed to make the transfer work?

7. What is deep linking? What have the U.S. courts said about its legality?

8. Suppose your Web site includes a navigation panel and a content frame. You check all links in the navigation panel to ensure that none points to an external Web site. Does that practice guarantee that your site will never frame a deep link? If not, why not?

9. One way to ensure that your Web site will never frame a deep link is to create a new browser window for each deep link. This strategy is somewhat controversial. Give two reasons why some people might object to this practice.

10. Explain why links that point to sites that in turn use frames are problematic.

☆ Hands-On Exercises

1. Find a Web site that uses frames and navigate to a page "deep" inside it. Break that page out of the frame. What is the page's URL? If you were to bookmark this URL, would accessing the page by itself be satisfactory? If not, why not? Try to find a frames-based site where the content pages do not stand up well on their own. Identify the URL for one of the content pages, and explain why it suffers when it is taken out of its frame.

2. Create a frameset Web page containing two frames. The frames should divide your page into two columns: the right column should be 100 pixels wide and the left column should occupy any remaining space. Insert a text file into the right-side frame and a graphic image into the left-side frame. Why is it a good idea to embed the image inside an .html file before you add it to the frame, even if the page should display only the image? (If you aren't sure, add the image to the SRC attribute directly and identify any problems.)

3. Using the two-frame frameset described in Exercise 2, create a three-frame display in which the new frame runs across the bottom edge of the browser window. The bottom frame should be exactly 20 pixels high and should dis-

play a single line of text against a yellow background. This third frame should not have a scroll bar. Can you add an identical copy of the frame to the top edge of the browser window without removing the bottom frame? How many `.html` files does this frame system use? Is this the smallest number of files needed? (Assume that your image file is embedded in an `.html` file.)

4. Using the frame system described in Exercise 2 or 3, add three links to the page containing the image. Point these links to `www.yahoo.com`, `home.cnet.com`, and `www.awl.com`. When a visitor clicks on the Yahoo! link, that page should appear inside your frame. When a visitor clicks on the CNet link, that page should appear in a new browser window. When a visitor clicks on the Addison Wesley Longman link, that page should break out of the frame system, but remain inside the existing browser window.

5. Create a Web page that is designed to defy any frame that tries to capture it. Using the frame system described in Exercise 2, 3, or 4, add a link to the content page pointing to the defiant page. What happens when you click the link to the defiant page? Can you design the defiant page so that it reroutes any links to your home page when someone tries to link to the page from inside a frame, while all other links are rewarded with the expected link content?

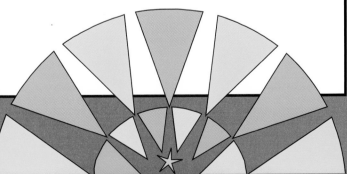

CHAPTER EIGHT

PUBLISHING ON THE WEB

Once you have finished designing and creating your Web pages, one final task remains. Each file must be transferred to a public Web server. You can perform these file transfers many ways, and the process will seem thoroughly straightforward once you become experienced with it. Unfortunately, some beginners stumble badly when they try to publish their first Web pages, so the process of installing Web pages on a Web server deserves careful attention. Consider the various options that are available, pick the one that seems easiest, and post your creations for public consumption.

◎◎ Chapter Objectives

☆ Run through a checklist of things to do before uploading a Web page

☆ Explain how to upload files using a Web browser

☆ Explain how to upload files using a Web page construction kit

☆ Explain how to upload files using an FTP client

☆ Explore some common troubleshooting scenarios

Get Ready: Seven Steps

Before you go public with your efforts, make sure that your Web pages are in good working order. A checklist of key points follows:

1. Page Check

First and foremost, view each Web page one final time with your Web browser. Confirm that your pages are readable, intelligible, and displayed correctly. In addition, you might check each page with both Microsoft Internet Explorer and Netscape Navigator. Consider running a spelling checker if you are prone to making spelling errors. Do everything possible to make your pages attractive, legible, and credible.

2. Link Check

Test the hyperlinks on all of your Web pages with a live Internet connection. Click each one to verify that it operates correctly. Also, make sure that your absolute links point to Web pages that aren't yours; links to your own pages should always be relative links.

3. JPEG Check

If you have any JPEG images, compress them to minimize download times.

4. IMG Check

Make sure that all of your `IMG` tags have `WIDTH`, `HEIGHT`, and `ALT` attributes.

5. Navigation Check

Make sure that you have enough in-site links to make navigation easy. Does every page contain a pointer back to your main page? Do all of your named anchor sections have return links back to the top of the page (or to a virtual table of contents)?

6. Point of Contact and Acknowledgments Check

Have you identified yourself on any of your pages? Did you give your readers an e-mail address where they can reach you? If your pages are informational, acknowledge all of your sources and supply links to related Web sites.

7. Copyright Statement Check

If you are posting original artwork or text that requires an explicit copyright statement, make sure that statement is easy to see and worded correctly.

Once your pages are ready to go, you need access to a Web server where you can store your files. That is, you need your own password-protected computer account on a computer that is set up to act as a Web server. Accounts with commercial Internet service providers typically include a Web server account offering approximately 10MB of free space for your Web pages. Alternatively, you may have a university account that includes space on a university Web server.

☆**TIP** **How the Pros Do It**

When a professional Web designer checks a Web site, he or she typically views each page with both Internet Explorer and Netscape Navigator on Macintosh and Windows computers and under a variety of monitor resolution settings (performing at least 12 separate tests for each page). In addition to checking for browser differences, the designer must view any colors that are not Web-safe at least four times just in case they do not "travel" well. A diligent professional will also run one or two older versions of each browser to verify that the pages do not depend too much on recent browser innovations. Because most people are not in a position to run all of these tests, sites designed by amateurs often present problems for at least some visitors. The pros are paid to do it right, however— and doing it right means lots of testing.

☆**SHORTCUT** **Web Page Testing Services**

If you aren't a professional Web designer but want to look like one, consider utilizing a Web page testing service. A good service will analyze your Web pages and identify any problems related to specific browsers. It will even specify what percentage of the Web viewing audience is likely to be affected by each problem. You can then decide whether you care enough to fix it.

Regardless of where you have access to a Web server, you need to know some crucial things about your server account: your user ID and password, the Web server's address, and the path to your Web directory on the Web server. You will also want to learn the URL for your home page.

Your User ID and Password

When you first set up your computer account, you are assigned a user ID and a password for that account. You will need these items to log on to the server. If you have forgotten either your user ID or password, contact the Help Desk for assistance. You must have this information before you can upload any files to the Web server.

The Host Address for Your Web Server

To upload files to a Web server, you need the host address for the Web server. This name is probably not the same host name seen in Web page URLs for that server. You cannot determine the host address by looking at URLs, but rather must (1) examine online documentation describing your computer privileges or (2) consult with Help Desk staff. You also need this information before attempting to upload any files to the Web server.

The Directory Path to Your Web Directory on the Web Server

After contacting your Web server, you must determine exactly where your public Web space resides in the hierarchy of Web server directories. Although this location can be described in terms of a directory path, it is probably *not* the exact same directory path seen in the URLs for that server (though they may be similar). Ideally, your software should be able to locate your home directory automatically, but sometimes this effort fails. If you need to supply the directory path manually, you can obtain the necessary path name by (1) examining online documentation describing your computer privileges or (2) consulting with Help Desk staff.

> ☆ **TIP**　**Directories for Web Pages**
>
> Each operating system has a slightly different way of organizing Web page directories. If your server runs the UNIX operating system, all of your Web pages will go into a directory named `public_html`, which is a subdirectory inside your home directory. If your server runs Windows NT, you must load your Web pages directly into your home directory (or any directories that you choose to create directly under your home directory). Most Web servers at educational institutions run UNIX.

The URL for Your Personal Home Page

After uploading your pages, you will want to tell people how to find those pages. Different servers use a variety of naming conventions for home page URLs. You should be able to obtain the correct URL for your personal home page by (1) examining online documentation or (2) asking Help Desk staff. You will need this information to check your Web pages after installing them on the Web server.

> ☆ **TIP**　**Free Web Server Space**
>
> Some Web sites offer users free space for their personal Web pages—but with a catch. "Free" Web page services tend to add a banner ad or a pop-up ad to your Web pages. To keep your pages clear of advertisements, you must obtain a personal account on a Web server that is not subsidized by advertising.

◎◎ Using Your Web Browser

One option for uploading your Web pages is to use your Web browser. This little-known technique is perfect for people who do not want to install additional software on their computer. No software beyond a Web browser is required. The only catch is that your Web browser supports file uploads in a "no frills" mode—that is, without the features or conveniences normally provided by other techniques. This uploading method works well for beginners, and everyone can start at this point and be happy. If you must update your Web site frequently, however, you will probably want to migrate to one of the other techniques at some point.

Web browsers normally use HTTP (Hypertext Transfer Protocol) connections to download Web pages, but they cannot employ such a connection to upload files to a Web server. Instead, to upload files to a Web server, you must first establish an FTP (File Transfer Protocol) connection with that server. You initiate an FTP connection by typing the appropriate address (that is, an address following the fixed formula described below) into your browser's location window. If you gathered all the information described in the last section, you are ready to establish an FTP connection using either Internet Explorer or Netscape Navigator.

Figure 8.1 shows the formula required to make an FTP connection. You should customize this formula with two key pieces of information: the user ID for your account and the host address for the Web server.

This address goes into the same location window normally reserved for Web page URLs, but note that you use an `ftp://` prefix instead of an `http://` pre-

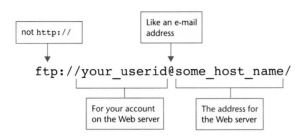

Figure 8.1 Type This Address into Your Browser's Location Window

fix. The prefix creates an FTP connection with the server instead of launching a request for a Web page. As soon as the Web server receives this FTP command, it responds with a password prompt (see Figure 8.2) because you are ready to access a personal computer account.

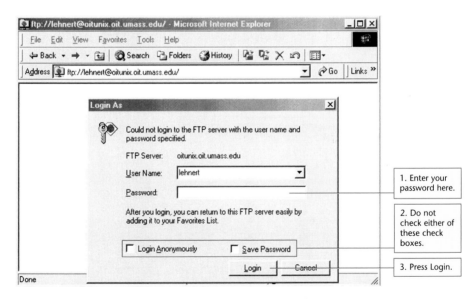

Figure 8.2 No One Accesses the Server without a Password

Once past the password gateway, you will have a live FTP connection with the Web server. You can easily recognize that the connection is working when your Web browser displays a list of files and directories (see Figure 8.3). When all goes well, your home directory on the Web server will be listed, and that directory will include a subdirectory (folder) named `public_html`. If you are not automatically dropped into your home directory, you can reach it by using the path name for your home directory. Once positioned in your home directory, look for a directory named `public_html`, which will hold all of your Web pages. If no `public_html` directory appears in your home directory, contact the Help Desk staff and ask them how to proceed.

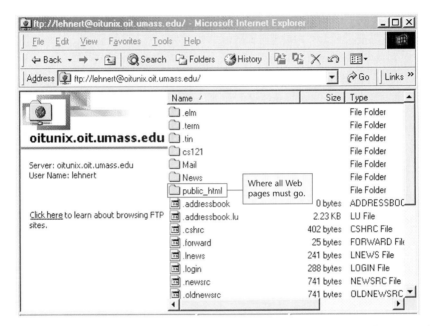

Figure 8.3 A Home Directory Display from Internet Explorer Running Under Microsoft Millennium Edition

---

☆ **SHORTCUT**   **Shortcut URLs**

On most Web servers, if the `public_html` directory contains a file named `index.html`, you can delete the portion of your URL that says `public_html/index.html`; the remaining URL will still allow you to reach your `index.html` file. On other servers, shortcuts may be associated with pages named `index.htm`, `default.html`, `default.htm`, `index.asp`, or `default.asp`. Check your server documentation or ask the Help Desk staff to find out which filenames are associated with shortcut URLs on your server.

Your home directory will look a little different from the one in Figure 8.3, but it should have a `public_html` directory in which you can store your Web page files. If you click the link for the `public_html` directory, you will see the files and directories in your `public_html` directory.

☆ **TIP**   **If You Get Lost**

If you cannot find your `public_html` directory, your FTP connection might not have brought up your home directory. Alternatively, you may be positioned in your home directory but the `public_html` directory hasn't been created yet. Although most Web server computer accounts are automatically configured to include a `public_html` directory, some are not. In any case, contact the Help Desk for assistance with your Web server account.

Next, you must decide where to install your Web page files. If all of them will be placed into `public_html`, then you are ready to upload your file. If the files will go in a different subdirectory, then you must create that subdirectory and path to it before uploading. Recall from Chapter Four that it is important to preserve the same directory structure used on your local host when you install your pages on a Web server. If your pages reside in multiple file folders on the computer where you developed your Web pages, then you must duplicate those folders (subdirectories) on the Web server. To create a new subdirectory on the Web server, pull down the File menu, select New, and then select Folder (see Figure 8.4).

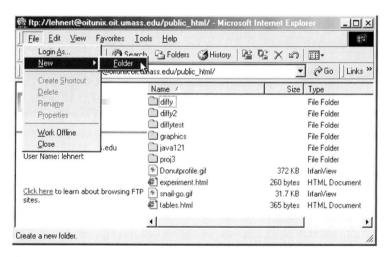

Figure 8.4 Creating a New Subdirectory on the Web Server

To change directories, click the subdirectory links in your browser window. If you need to reach the directory above the current directory, you can either click the Back button or look for a link named "Up to higher-level directory." On some directory displays, this link may contain only two periods "..". In either case, you will always find this link (if it exists) listed at the top of the directory display.

When you are ready to upload a file, you must deal with the quirks of Netscape Navigator and Internet Explorer.

☆WARNING **Some Browsers Can't Create New Directories**

If you need to create new directories on the Web server, some browsers can help you—but some cannot. If your browser does not offer a New Folder or New Directory command, you must use one of the other uploading options.

Netscape Navigator

Once you have reached the directory where you want to install a Web page file, open the File menu and click Upload File. A dialog box will appear, allowing you to locate the file that will be uploaded on your hard drive. Select the file you want, and send it to the server.

Internet Explorer

Instead of moving into the directory where you want to install a Web page file, stay in the parent directory and highlight the directory where your file should go. On the File menu, select Copy To Folder (see Figure 8.5). A dialog box will appear, allowing you to locate the file you want to upload on your hard drive. Select the file you want, and send it to the server.

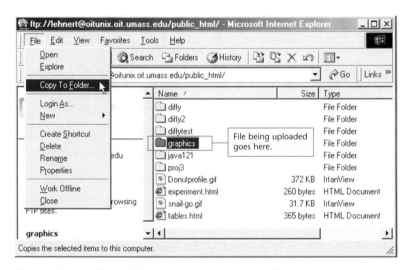

Figure 8.5 Uploading a File from Internet Explorer's File Menu

☆SHORTCUT   **Drag and Drop Your Files onto the Web Server**

If your Web page files are present on your desktop or in an open folder, you can upload them to the Web server by dragging and dropping file icons from your desktop onto the browser's directory display window. The drag-and-drop method is convenient when you have several files to upload. To drag more than one file at a time, hold down the Shift key, click the desired file icons, and drag the whole bunch into the browser window. All of the files will then be uploaded. Both Navigator and Internet Explorer support drag-and-drop file uploads (see Figure 8.6).

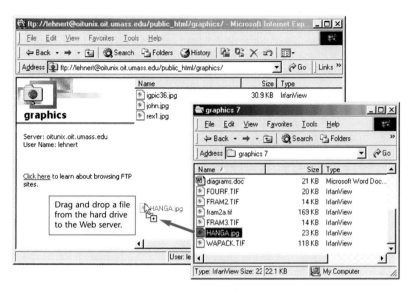

Figure 8.6 Uploading a File from Internet Explorer's File Menu

Once the file upload is complete, the directory display will be updated and the new file should be visible in the Web server's directory display. If you cannot see the file on the Web server, the uploading operation failed.

☆**WARNING Close Your FTP Connection**

When your file uploads are finished, exit your browser to terminate your FTP session. This step is especially important if other people have access to your computer (for example, in an office environment). As long as the current browser session is active, anyone can access your Web pages on the Web server. An unscrupulous person could then delete your Web pages, replace them with different Web pages, or engage in other forms of mischief to teach you a lesson.

◎◉ Using a Web Page Construction Kit

HTML construction kits generally include a publishing feature that allows you to upload your Web pages to a Web server. In this section, we will investigate how Netscape Communicator's Composer uploads files. Composer is a simple Web page construction kit that is included in the Communicator software suite. Other construction kits publish Web pages in a similar fashion.

Your first step is to launch Composer from the Communicator menu. (*Note*: Even if you've created your Web pages without Composer, you can still use Composer to upload them to a Web server.) Next, follow these steps:

1. From the File menu, select Open Page and then use the directory dialog box to locate the HTML file to be uploaded.

2. From the File menu, select Publish. Figure 8.7 shows the window that pops up at this time.

3. Fill in all of the fields in the pop-up window.

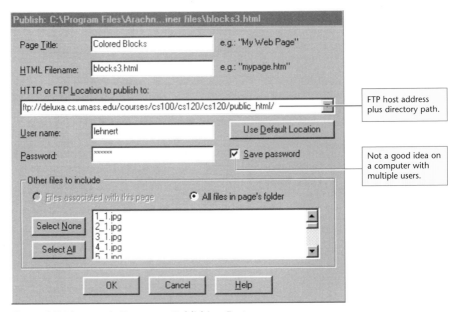

Figure 8.7 Netscape's Composer Publishing Feature

If you open a Web page before reaching this pop-up window, the first two fields in step 3 will be filled in automatically. In the third field, called "HTTP or FTP Location to publish to," enter the server address, including the directory path to your `public_html` directory on the Web server. Add the `ftp://` prefix to complete the destination address. Once you've entered this information, it becomes a default; Composer will fill it in automatically when you next upload Web pages. Your user ID and password go into the next two boxes. Check the Save password check box to save these entries so that you won't have to enter them again; do not select this option if you share your computer with someone else.

Composer includes a convenient feature that makes it easy to upload groups of related files all at once. If other files appear in the same subdirectory as your current page (the page open inside Composer), you can opt to load all of them simultaneously along with the current page. Thus, if your whole Web site is found in one subdirectory, you can upload the entire site by clicking the All files in page's folder button and then clicking OK. Alternatively, you might opt to upload only the files that are referenced by the current page via links on the current page. Composer gives you two different ways to initiate multiple file uploads.

☆WARNING **File Uploads Overwrite Old Files**

If your Web server already contains a file with the same filename as one of the files that you are uploading, *the file being uploaded will automatically overwrite the file on the server.* You will not see any warnings, and you will not be asked whether you want to overwrite the old file; it will just happen. Once you upload a file and overwrite an existing file, you won't be able to recover the original if you have made a mistake.

◎◎ Using an FTP Client

You can also upload files to a Web server with a general-purpose FTP client. You will need the same information as when you use the other uploading techniques, but in many ways you combine the best of browser uploads and construction kit uploads. For example, you can reach the correct Web page directory by clicking each subdirectory along the way, as in the browser approach; this approach is usually easier than typing in the complete path name (as shown in Figure 8.7). In addition, you can save crucial information for future sessions, as in the construction kit approach. A good FTP client should provide the best possible combination of uploading features.

You can download many good FTP clients from the Internet, often for free. WS_FTP, the most popular client for Windows, comes in both freeware (lite) and shareware (pro) versions. The most popular FTP client for the Mac is Fetch, another free program (see Figure 8.8).

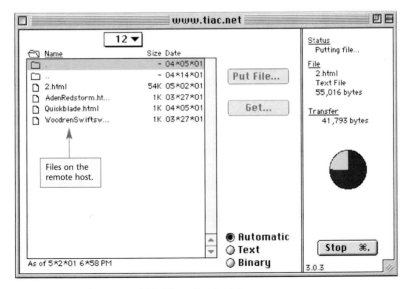

Figure 8.8 Fetch—A Free FTP Client for the Mac

Figure 8.9 shows an FTP client named LeechFTP, which supports drag-and-drop file transfers between its two directory displays. It also lets you save multiple server session configurations (for example, your user ID, password, and a default directory).

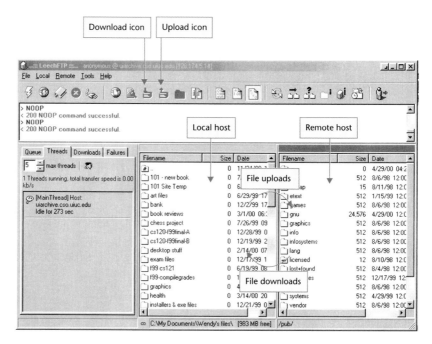

Figure 8.9 Most FTP Clients Display Both Local and Remote Directories

---

☆ **TIP** **Text, Binary, and Automated File Transfer Options**

Most FTP clients have a setting that you must check before executing an upload command. All file transfers must be performed in either text mode or binary mode (for text files and binary files, respectively). Many FTP clients will attempt to figure out which kind of file is being transferred based on the file extension; these clients offer an automated option in addition to the text and binary options. As long as you use common file types (such as `.html` or `.jpg`), you can choose the automated option.

◎◎ Troubleshooting

After moving your Web page files onto a Web server, you need to check them on the server. Once you've performed thorough page checks (that is, looking at all of your pages and testing all of your links) a few times, spot checks should be adequate. As a beginner, you should check your pages carefully as soon as they appear on the Web server. Unfortunately, all sorts of annoying gremlins can pop up after you move your files to a Web server—especially while you are still learning.

The URL for Your Web Page Doesn't Work (404 Not Found Errors)

Four possible errors may have occurred to cause this situation.

1. Your URL contains an error.

Solution: Check for typographical errors, case errors, and similar problems in the entry in the location box. Double-check your URL with your Web server's Help Desk to confirm that it is correct.

2. You uploaded to the wrong directory.

Solution: Check your directory listings on the Web server to locate the file.

3. Your filename was altered during the upload process.

Solution: See Case 2 in the section called "Hyperlinks Don't Work Anymore."

4. You never uploaded the file referenced in the URL—perhaps the upload failed.

Solution: Try again.

Hyperlinks Don't Work Anymore (404 Not Found Errors)

Check for three possibilities in this situation.

1. If a hyperlink worked on your local host but doesn't work on the Web server, it is probably a relative URL and hence is sensitive to its location in the local directory structure.

Solution: Verify that the Web page containing the URL was installed in the correct subdirectory. Next, check the target Web page and confirm that page was installed in the correct subdirectory. Also, make sure that you haven't changed the overall directory structure of your site. The exact same set of directories on your local host must be faithfully replicated on the Web server, preserving all subdirectory relationships exactly as they existed on your local host.

2. Sometimes the software that uploads your Web files alters filenames so that the filenames on the server no longer match the filenames on your local host.

Solution: Examine your directories on the Web server and check the filenames listed there. Do they match the filenames on your local host? Watch for changes in case—these filenames are case-sensitive, so each character in the hyperlink's filename must exactly match the corresponding character in the Web server's filename (that is, uppercase-to-uppercase and lowercase-to-lowercase matching). If you find a mismatch, you can edit the filename on the server (some FTP clients make this change as easy as editing a filename in Windows Explorer), or you can modify the filename in the hyperlink and then reload the Web page containing that link.

3. Make sure that no absolute URL points to a page on your local host.

Solution: Absolute URLs for pages on your local host start with a `file://` prefix instead of an `http://` prefix. An example of an absolute URL on a local host follows:

```
file:///C|/My Documents/Wendy's files/cs121/quizzes/
sp01-1.htm
```

Absolute links to a page on a local host may work when you view them on that particular local host, but they won't work when you try to view them from another host. In particular, they will fail when you try to follow them from a Web server. If your Web pages include any of these links, convert them to relative URLs (see Chapter Four).

Hyperlinks Don't Work Anymore (Forbidden Access Errors)

With a little luck, you will never encounter one of these errors. When they do occur, you'll see a statement that says something about file permissions:

```
You don't have permission to access project1.htm
on this server.
```

Solution: If this type of error arises after you've uploaded your Web pages, contact your Web server's Help Desk for assistance. You can fix the problem yourself, but you need software that can change UNIX protection codes; the exact procedure depends on the software you use to upload your files. Sometimes Help Desk personnel will step in and correct the flaw for you. Most Web servers do not require Web page authors to make their own file protection adjustments. With a little luck, you will never have to deal with this type of error.

Image Files Aren't Displaying

You see box with a red X or a question mark instead of your image.

Solution: Problems with image files are analogous to problems with hyperlinks (see the "Hyperlinks Don't Work Anymore" section). Check the same scenarios described for problem hyperlinks. Also check for typographical errors in your attribute name (for example, make sure that you didn't type SCR instead of SRC).

☆ **TIP**   **Image Display Errors**

If you see a red X (in Internet Explorer) or a question mark (in Netscape Navigator) instead of an image, put your mouse over the area where the image should be, right-click, and select View Image. The resulting error message will indicate whether the problem is a "404 Not Found" error or a "Forbidden Access" error.

☆ Summary

▷ Before publishing your Web pages, analyze them by completing a quality-control checklist and make modifications as needed.

▷ Although many ways to upload Web pages to a server exist, you always need some core information about your server before starting the uploading process.

▷ You can upload Web pages with a Web browser, a Web page construction kit, or an FTP client.

▷ It is important to check your pages carefully after each upload until you gain enough experience to be completely confident with the process. Many things can go wrong, especially when you are a beginner.

▷ Consult a troubleshooting list when things go wrong.

☆ Online References

Evaluating Web Resources (Add These Checklists to Your Publishing Checklist)
`http://www2.widener.edu/Wolfgram-Memorial-Library/webevaluation/webeval.htm`

Web Site Garage (Free One-Page Tune-Up)
`http://websitegarage.netscape.com/O=wsg/`

CAST Bobby (Page Testing for Special Browser Accessibility)
`http://www.cast.org/bobby/`

A Download Site for WS_FTP Limited Edition (for Windows)
`http://www.ipswitch.com/cgi/download_eval.pl?product=WL-1000`

LeechFTP Downloads (for Windows)
`http://stud.fh-heilbronn.de/~jdebis/leechftp/downloads.html`

Fetch Softworks (an FTP Client for Macs)
`http://fetchsoftworks.com/`

☆ Review Questions

1. Name three types of software that you can use to upload Web pages.

2. Are "free" Web servers really free? Explain your answer.

3. Suppose you have a personal computer account on a Web browser named `elwood.student.univ.edu` with user ID = `smith` and password = `f56Wimpy`, and you want to establish an FTP connection using a Web browser. What address should you type into your browser's location window?

4. Why is the filename `index.html` special?

155

5. Can a Web browser upload more than one file at a time? If so, how?

6. Name one thing that you can do when uploading files with Composer that you cannot do with a Web browser.

7. When is it a bad idea to let your uploading software remember your password?

8. Why might you need to create new directories (folders) on the Web server?

9. Describe three ways that hyperlink "404 Not Found" errors can arise on Web servers.

10. Which file errors are more common: "404 Not Found" errors or "Forbidden Permission" errors? Which ones can you correct without any knowledge of UNIX?

☆ Hands-On Exercises

All of these exercises require access to a Web server.

1. Upload a file named `index.html` to a Web server and display it using a shortcut URL in your browser's location window.

2. Upload an `.html` file that contains an image but don't upload the corresponding image file. Display the `.html` file (on the server) using your Web browser. Describe what appears where the image should be. Now upload the image file and reload the Web page. Does the image display correctly? If not, figure out what's wrong and fix your Web page.

3. Display your home directory via an FTP connection using your Web browser. Work your way up the directory hierarchy of the Web server by clicking the parent directory links. What is the name of the highest directory that you can view? Try accessing other subdirectories from the top parent directory. Can you see all of them? If not, what error do you receive when you try to view certain directories?

4. Display a Web page directory (for example, `public_html` if it exists) using an FTP connection to your personal Web browser. Will your Web browser allow you to bookmark this address? If not, copy and paste the address to a text file. Exit your browser, restart your browser, and then return to the FTP address (either by using a bookmark or by pasting the address in your location window). What happens when you try to return to this address?

5. Sometimes Web server directories are configured so that you can view them with a Web browser and a public `http://` address (not an FTP connection). Create a Web page subdirectory on your Web server, upload an `.html` file to this directory, and display that new page using an `http://` URL. Next, remove the filename part of the URL and try to load the resulting URL. What does your browser return? (There are two possibilities—you will see either a directory listing or an error message.) If you see a directory listing, does it contain any hyperlinks? If so, describe them. If you see an error message, what kind of error is it?

APPENDIX A: COPYRIGHT LAWS

What Is a Copyright?

The Web is a communications medium where anyone can distribute written words, recorded music, photographs, and images of all kinds, including videos. If you have added intellectual property to your Web page that is not your own, you may be guilty of a copyright infringement. If you haven't taken the time to learn about copyright law and its application to Web publishing, you may be setting yourself up for a possible lawsuit. Read on.

A **copyright** confers certain rights and privileges to its owner. Copyrights are normally granted to the author of a written work or to an artist, musician, or anyone who creates some original "intellectual property." Prior to April 1, 1989, explicit declarations of copyright ownership were required on written documents to afford copyright protections. The law has since changed, however. Now all works created after April 1, 1989, are automatically copyrighted and protected, regardless of whether they contain a copyright notice. If a document lacks an explicit copyright notice, you should assume that standard copyright protections apply anyway.

A **copyright infringement** is any action that violates the legal rights of a copyright owner. All copyright infringements are illegal, but not all infringements result in legal actions. It is the responsibility of the owner of the copyright to initiate retaliatory actions, which typically take the form of a civil lawsuit.

Even when works are distributed for free on the Web, they are still subject to copyright restrictions. Although one Web site may have been granted distributed rights, that does not mean that everyone enjoys those same distribution rights. For example, just because you may be granted the right to download an image or an audio file at no charge, you cannot necessarily redistribute that file without obtaining permission to do so from the copyright holder.

Many people believe that they can't be sued for a copyright infringement if they do not derive any personal profit from the property under contention. Any distribution of a document, image, or sound recording, however, might undermine the potential for a profitable print distribution, which could be assessed in terms of lost income to the copyright owner. Digital distributions hold the greatest potential for damage because no one can halt the distribution once it has begun. It is irrelevant that you didn't profit from the distribution: the only profit that matters is the one that the copyright owner lost.

Personal Use

When a work has been legally obtained by an individual, that person has a right to enjoy the work within certain boundaries. These boundaries apply to all copyrighted works, whether they were obtained for a price or downloaded for free from an authorized distribution site on the Web. For the purposes of this discussion, we will focus on documents, images, and audio files that have been legally obtained over the Internet.

Printing Text Documents and Pictures

If you print one copy of a text document or picture for your own personal use, no problem arises. If you want to print copies for friends and the material does not contain an explicit statement about allowable distributions, you must obtain permission from the author or whoever owns the copyright before duplicating the material.

Storing Text Documents, Pictures, and Audio Files

You can download and retain a copy of a legally obtained text document, picture, or audio file, provided that you don't distribute the file to others or make it publicly available. Keep in mind that the author of the work no longer controls your copy. If you intend to reference a text document or quote from it at a later time, you should always locate the most up-to-date version, in case the author has made updates, corrections, or any other alterations.

Making Copies of Web Pages

You are allowed to retain a copy of a Web page for personal use, but you cannot redistribute the file either digitally or in print unless the Web page explicitly grants that permission. If you want to share a Web page with a friend, send an e-mail message to your friend giving the appropriate URL. This is the correct way to share Web pages without violating the rights of Web page authors.

Copying and Modifying Text Documents

When you alter text that isn't yours, you must be extremely careful to acknowledge the extent of your alterations and the source of the original document. Some authors suggest that the altered file be identified as a "heavily edited modification of an original source document by so-and-so, which can be found at such-and-such a location."

If you alter someone else's file and present it as your own, you may or may not be violating copyright laws, depending on how much original material survives verbatim. In any event, you are probably guilty of **plagiarism**. Plagiarism occurs when you adopt the substance of someone else's work, rewrite it in your own words, and fail to give proper credit to the original source. If you present the substance of someone else's words, be sure to identify and acknowledge the original source. No laws against plagiarism exist, but plagiarism is not tolerated in professional circles. In an academic environment, plagiarism is considered a form of academic dishonesty and is grounds for serious disciplinary action.

Copying and Modifying HTML Source Code

Modifications of source code are subject to different rules than modifications of written text. If you download the HTML version of a Web page because you like the page's format, you may retain all of the HTML commands and substitute your own content into the HTML framework, without permission or acknowledgments. The "look and feel" of a computer screen is not protected by copyright or patent; it can be freely duplicated without permission. As long as you substitute your own content, you have not violated any copyright restrictions and you are not plagiarizing any material. Indeed, this strategy provides an easy way to create a sophisticated Web page as well as an honorable way to learn HTML.

◎◎ Explicit Permissions

Authors can license specific rights to the general public by including a statement describing the rights and privileges being granted. For example, a Web page might include a statement such as the following:

Permission is granted to freely copy (unmodified) this document in electronic form or in print as long as you're not selling it. On the World Wide Web, however, you must link here rather than put it on your own page.

Such a statement effectively allows anyone to reproduce and post an exact copy of the document online in almost any fashion. It explicitly prohibits the use of mirrored Web pages (copies of the original Web pages posted on different Web servers), however.

Another commonly encountered copyright provision reads as follows:

This work may be redistributed freely, in whole or in part, but cannot be sold or used for profit or as part of a product or service that is sold for profit.

If the Web page does not include a statement such as this one, you must assume that no such privileges apply. When a copyright provision allows for redistribution without permission, you still must identify the author, source, and publisher (if one exists) in all distributions of the original work.

When a copyright owner grants explicit permissions to the general public, some restrictions may be relaxed while other restrictions remain in force. On the Internet, for example, you will often encounter copyright provisions that permit redistributions as long as you do not charge a fee for the material. Other provisions permit redistribution only if you included certain identifying information in the redistribution and do not modify the original document in any way. A copyright owner can revoke explicit permissions at any time, although it may be difficult to reverse digital distributions of materials once they have been allowed.

A Web page author may grant explicit permissions to the general public through published provisions or to specific individuals and companies through licensing agreements. For example, publishers routinely request and obtain explicit permission to use photographs and other materials in books and magazines. Permission to use protected materials may be granted in exchange for a licensing fee, a specified acknowledgment, or both.

Permission to Add Photographs or Cartoons to a Web Site

If you find a photograph or a cartoon in a newspaper, magazine, or book, you cannot simply scan the image and add it to your Web page unless you track down the copyright holder and secure written permission to do so. The copyright owner might be the photographer or artist, a wire service (in the case of a photograph), or the publisher. Photographs and drawings are protected by copyright restrictions, in the same way that written text is protected. For example, Playboy Enterprises sued the Event Horizons BBS for distributing unauthorized digital copies of Playboy photographs. Its lawsuit resulted in a $500,000 fine against Event Horizons.

Images found on the Web are subject to the same legal restrictions and requirements. Because many people copy and redistribute graphics files across the Web without obtaining the proper copyright permissions, there is an excellent chance that any graphic you find on someone else's Web page has already been posted without permission and is being used illegally. This is especially likely to be the case with professional photographs. A responsible Web page author will attempt to locate the rightful owner of the graphic and secure permission to use it.

Permission to Add Hyperlinks to a Web Site

Hypertext makes it easy to connect one Web site to another Web site or a portion of a Web site. You normally do not need permission to add hyperlinks to other Web pages, although some restrictions apply.

Some Web page authors ask that all hyperlinks reference their pages at some "top-level" entry point. That is, they don't want you to set up a link to a secondary page if that page wasn't designed to be a self-contained, stand-alone page. When a Web page author explicitly makes such a request, you should respect it. Even if no explicit linking prohibition is present, it makes sense to link to top-level entry points in large Web sites for practical reasons. For instance, Web masters who maintain large Web sites occasionally rearrange the site's pages and rename files. If you reference a secondary page directly, your link might become obsolete during such a reorganization. If you always reference the main entry to a Web site and identify the links needed to get to a secondary page, your hyperlink is far less likely to require an update when the Web master alters the other site.

The practice of creating links to interior segments of a larger Web site or individual elements of specific Web pages is called **deep linking**. For example, it is always possible to add an image from another Web site to your Web page by creating an IMG SCR attribute with an absolute URL to the original image file. This idea may seem attractive because it does not involve making any unauthorized copies of the image. Plus, creating a link to the original image preserves the author's control over that image. Unfortunately, this practice has other drawbacks. In particular, downloading a graphic file from a third-party Web server consumes more bandwidth than a link to a file on the local server. You are also consuming the resources of someone else's server whenever someone downloads your Web page. Most importantly from a copyright perspective, you have altered the context in which the image appears. The owner of the image might want to control the surrounding context (for example, any captions under the image). He or she should have the right to withhold permission for you to include the image on your Web site, depending on the way you intend to use it.

A similar deep linking problem arises in the context of frames. When a Web page points to an external Web site from inside a frame, it may not be apparent to the user that the page inside the frame is not part of the original site. Indeed, a number of lawsuits have already arisen over the practice of deep linking in this context. If you intend to link to an external Web site inside a frame, you should always obtain permission from the other Web site. The courts have consistently sided with the site that is framed—not with the site doing the framing (see Chapter Seven for more about frames and deep linking).

Permission to Add Web Pages to a Web Site

Adding a hyperlink to someone else's Web page is very different from adding a copy of a Web page to your own site. Although you do not normally need permission to link to another Web site (the exceptions to this rule were described earlier in this appendix), you should never copy someone else's Web page and then link to your copy. When you link to the author's original page, the author retains control over that page. If he or she wants to update, correct, or modify it in any way, your site will automatically benefit from that effort because your hyperlink always points to the most recent version of the author's page. If you link to your own copy of someone else's page, however, you cannot know whether that page is up to date or obsolete, because you have removed it from the hands of the author. All absolute hyperlinks respect the will of other Web page authors to control the content of their own Web pages. If a Web page author removes a page from the Web, any hyperlinks to that page will become obsolete—but removing the page is always the author's prerogative.

◎◎ Public Domain

An author can renounce and relinquish all copyright privileges for an original work by placing the work in the **public domain**. For example, the author may issue a proclamation that says something like, "I grant this work to the public domain." Conversely, works that have not been explicitly released to the public domain cannot enter the public domain while the author remains alive. After an author has died, his or her heirs or publisher may renew the author's copyrights for another 70 years. Once an author has been dead for 70 years, any materials by that person automatically enter into the public domain. This fact explains why older novels and books can be (re)published and distributed more cheaply than current fiction.

Material in the public domain can be distributed freely in both electronic and print form. Nevertheless, you should not assume that a work is in the public domain simply because it is popular or ubiquitous. For example, the song "Happy Birthday" is not in the public domain.

◎◎ The Fair Use Doctrine

Once you understand that restrictions apply to what you can and cannot do with text and graphics that you find online, you will be pleased to discover that some standard practices and conventions allow you to freely incorporate portions of someone else's work into your own. Moreover, if you stay within commonly accepted guidelines, you do not need to obtain anyone's permission before embellishing your own efforts with the words or artistry of others. The guidelines that sanction such privileges are called **fair use guidelines**, and they are protected by a legal doctrine called the **doctrine of fair use**.

The doctrine of fair use allows writers and scholars to refer to other works by quoting excerpts from them. This reuse is typically employed to argue a point, to present evidence, or for the sake of illustration. To quote from a copyrighted work, you must follow certain rules of thumb. If you research the concept of fair use, you will probably find different guidelines, because no absolute legal guidelines exist— only conventions. Widely accepted conventions are safe to use, but be prepared to be flexible if people object to your use of their materials. In this spirit, we provide some rules of thumb for occasions when you are working with text that is not your own.

☆**TIP**   **Specific Guidelines for Text**

You may quote 300 words from a book or 150 words from a magazine or newspaper article as long as you observe the following guidelines:

☆ The excerpt is not a complete unit in the larger work (for example, a complete poem, a complete article, or a complete list of rules from a manual).

☆ The excerpt represents less than 20% of the original work.

☆ The excerpt is integrated into your own writing and does not stand alone as a self-contained section or chapter opening.

☆ You give full credit to the author, source, and publisher.

Before quoting a personal e-mail message, a Web page, or an unpublished document, you must obtain permission from the author.

Before reproducing any illustrations, photographs, or any portion of a copyrighted video or audio file, you must obtain permission from the copyright owner.

Note that *ideas* cannot be copyrighted; rather, the *specific arrangement of words* used to express an idea is the object of copyright protections. Also, copyright protections apply only to text that is quoted verbatim. You are always free to summarize or restate the content of any work in your own writings. Of course, a summation of someone else's work without proper acknowledgment is plagiarism. Always acknowledge a source if you are drawing detailed information from that source.

If an explicit statement prohibits the distribution of an excerpt that normally would be justified under the fair use doctrine, the doctrine of fair use cannot be applied. For example, suppose that the following prohibition appears in an online document:

No part of this electronic publication can be reproduced or retransmitted without the prior written permission of the publisher.

In this case, you cannot excerpt this work without obtaining the author's consent.

Alternatively, suppose you encounter a document that contains the notation "Do Not Quote." In that case, you cannot reproduce any excerpts from the material. Explicit restrictions always override default conventions.

The application of copyright law to the Internet has created a legal quagmire, and many competing special interests are at stake. Ignorance of the law is never a good defense, nor is the notion of safety in numbers (as in, "Hey, everyone else is doing it"). If you must take risks with copyright law, don't say we didn't warn you.

๑๑ Copyright Law in a Digital Era

When you consider the rights and restrictions that apply to online text, think about how easily a text document can be distributed in digital form. If someone posts a document to a mailing list, it might be accessible through an archive for years to come. Copies of it might be mirrored at countless Web sites and redistributed repeatedly via e-mail. In such a case, if the original author wants to correct an error in the original document or revise it with important updates, recalling all of the copies of the original version will be impossible. The author no longer controls the document in the same way that a publisher can control print editions of a book.

Everyone benefits when authors retain maximal control over the digital distribution of their documents. Stricter control offers the only way to minimize the propagation of misinformation or outdated information. In addition, it gives everyone access to the best-quality information online. In the interest of effective online communication, you must be sensitive to the rights of authors, no matter where a document was originally posted or how limited its potential scope might be. With 150 million people online, it's impossible to predict the digital trajectory of an online document.

In October 1998, the **Digital Millennium Copyright Act (DMCA)** was signed into law in an effort to strengthen intellectual property rights on the Web. This law protects an Internet service provider (ISP) from liability for any copyright infringements on its Web servers, as long as the ISP has no prior knowledge of the infringement. In return for this protection, all ISPs (commercial and otherwise) must maintain a DMCA agent who responds to complaints about potential copyright violations. Once a copyright owner registers a complaint, the acting DMCA agent must disable online access to the material in question. In other words, Web pages can be removed from Web servers without warning when they are called into question under the DMCA.

The DCMA protects both copyright owners and Web page authors from the possibility of hasty legal action. Nevertheless, all Web page authors must understand the possible consequences of casual copyright infringements. Use clip art and the fonts on your Web pages with care. If you are not authorized to redistribute them, your Web pages could be yanked from your ISP's server. It's too early to say how the DCMA will affect the growth of the Web or the ISPs, which must now respond to all copyright infringement complaints. Clearly, we are past the point of "anything goes" with respect to copyright infringement on the Web.

APPENDIX B: ONLINE RESOURCES

Chapter One (General HTML Resources)

HTML Goodies (lots of good tutorials for beginners)
`http://htmlgoodies.earthweb.com/`

Web Design Group (a friendly HTML resource for beginners)
`http://www.htmlhelp.com/`

WebMonkey (an online magazine for beginners and beyond)
`http://www.webmonkey.com/`

HTML Design I (a comprehensive clearinghouse for online resources)
`http://www.devs.com/zresources/html.html`

HTML Editors and Associated Tools (mostly for Windows)
`http://webdevelopersjournal.com/software/html_editors.html`

Top HTML Editors for the Mac (suitable for both beginners and professionals)
`http://macworld.zdnet.com/netsmart/features/editorintro.html`

HyperText Markup Language Home Page (from the W3C)
`http://www.w3.org/MarkUp`

HTML Validation Service
`http://validator.w3.org/file-upload.html`

Chapter Two (CSS, XML, and Other HTML-Related Topics)

Names for Colors (all safe for Internet Explorer and Navigator)
`http://users.rcn.com/giant.interport/COLOR/1ColorSpecifier.html`

A Reference Page for Special Characters
`http://www.ramsch.org/martin/uni/fmi-hp/iso8859-1.html`

CSS Quick Tutorial
`http://www.htmlhelp.com/reference/css/quick-tutorial.html`

Mulder's Stylesheets Tutorial
`http://hotwired.lycos.com/webmonkey/authoring/stylesheets/tutorials/tutorial1.html`

The Web Isn't for Everyone ... Yet
`http://hotwired.lycos.com/webmonkey/design/site_building/tutorials/tutorial5.html`

XHTML: What Exactly Is This Thing?
`http://htmlgoodies.earthweb.com/tutors/xhtml.html`

What Is XML?
`http://www.htmlgoodies.com/tutors/xml.html`

◎◎ Chapter Three (Color and Image Resources)

Color Charts
http://www.hypersolutions.org/rgb.html

A Tutorial on Hexadecimal Notation
http://hotwired.lycos.com/webmonkey/97/17/index2a.html

RGB versus RYB
http://home.pacbell.net/dbldgt/electronics/theory/light/
rgbryb001.html

Names for Colors (Recognized by Internet Explorer and Navigator)
http://users.rcn.com/giant.interport/COLOR/
1ColorSpecifier.html

Death of the Web-Safe Color Palette?
http://hotwired.lycos.com/webmonkey/00/37/
index2a.html?tw=design

Dazzling Graphics for the Web
http://palfrey.userworld.com/dazzle/outline.html

Images for Web Pages
http://www.stars.com/Graphics/Images/

Graphics Software
http://www.cs.ubc.ca/spider/ladic/software.html

FreeFoto.com
http://www.freefoto.com/

◎◎ Chapter Four (Links and Web Hosting)

Using Relative URLs
http://www.stack.nl/%7Egalactus/html/urls.html

Web Structure
http://www.matcmp.sunynassau.edu/~glassr/html/url.htm

Troubleshooting Broken Image Links (and Hyperlinks)
http://www.hostingmanual.net/forum/Support/12.shtml

Alert LinkRunner
http://www.alertbookmarks.com/lr/

LinkAlarm Web Service for Eliminating Broken Links
http://www.linkalarm.com/

Network Solutions WHOIS (domain name lookup)
http://networksolutions.com/cgi-bin/whois/whois

TopHosts.com-The Complete Web Hosting Resource
http://www.TopHosts.com/

◎◎ Chapter Five (Image File Formats and Tools)

LZW and GIF Explained
`http://www.msg.net/utility/whirlgif/lzw.html`

The GIF Controversy: A Software Developer's Perspective
`http://www.cloanto.com/users/mcb/19950127giflzw.html`

PNG (Portable Network Graphics)
`http://www.libpng.org/pub/png/`

MediaBuilder GIFWorks
`http://ruel.net/graphics/index.htm?`

Correct and Beautiful Transparent GIFs with Photoshop
`http://www.webdesignclinic.com/ezine/v1i2/trans/`

Animated GIFs from WebDeveloper.com
`http://webdeveloper.com/animations/`

Getting into Motion: A Guide for Adding Animation to Your Web Pages
`http://webdeveloper.com/design/design_getting_motion.html`

Constructing Animations (a tutorial)
`http://member.aol.com/royalef/gifmake.htm`

GIF Animators
`http://animation.about.com/arts/animation/cs/gifanimators/index.htm`

Streaming Media World
`http://streamingmediaworld.com`

◎◎ Chapter Six (Tables)

Page Layout, Margins, Indenting, and Columns (from hacks to style sheets)
`http://wdvl.com/Authoring/Design/Layout/index.html`

Using Tables for Web Site Layout (contains a discussion of table width and monitor resolution)
`http://www.webdevelopersjournal.com/diary/10_24.html`

The Not-So-Basic Table (a good explanation of **CELLPADDING** versus **CELLSPACING**)
`http://hotwired.lycos.com/webmonkey/96/48/index2a.html?tw=authoring`

Tables: W3C Recommendation (More about attributes)
`http://www.w3.org/TR/REC-html40/struct/tables.html`

Create Tables That Transform Gracefully (Problems with using tables as layout devices)
`http://www.w3.org/TR/WAI-WEBCONTENT/#gl-table-markup`

Tables on Non-table Browsers (a discussion of tabular tables for Lynx and other some browsers)
`http://ppewww.ph.gla.ac.uk/~flavell/www/tablejob.html`

◎◎ Chapter Seven (Frames)

Mikodocs Guide to HTML: Frames
`http://www.idocs.com/tags/frames/frames.html`

Frames Are a Picnic
`http://www.hotwired.com/webmonkey/html/96/31/index3a.html`

Fun with Frames
`http://www.builder.com/Authoring/Frames/`

HTML 4.0: Frames
`http://htmlgoodies.earthweb.com/tutors/html4_frames.html`

Using Inline Frames
`http://www.pageresource.com/html/iframe.htm`

Judge Rules on Deep Linking
`http://dgl.com/itinfo/2000/it000330.html`

Thinking About Linking
`http://www.llrx.com/features/weblink1.htm`

Deep Linking: Its Future on the Web
`http://www.internet-law-firm.com/articles/`
`Deep%20linking%20Its%20future%20on%20the%20Web.htm`

◎◎ Chapter Eight (Publishing Web Pages)

Evaluating Web Resources (add these checklists to your publishing checklist)
`http://www2.widener.edu/Wolfgram-Memorial-Library/`
`webevaluation/webeval.htm`

Web Site Garage (free one-page tune-up)
`http://websitegarage.netscape.com/O=wsg/`

CAST Bobby (page testing for special browser accessibility)
`http://www.cast.org/bobby/`

Download Site for WS_FTP Limited Edition (for Windows)
`http://www.ipswitch.com/cgi/download_eval.pl?product=WL-1000`

LeechFTP Downloads (for Windows)
`http://stud.fh-heilbronn.de/~jdebis/leechftp/downloads.html`

Fetch Softworks (an FTP client for Macs)
`http://fetchsoftworks.com/`

APPENDIX C: HTML TAGS AND ATTRIBUTES

The following table of HTML tags and tag attributes does not constitute a comprehensive listing of all HTML 4 elements, but it does cover the elements described in this book.

HTML Element	Attributes	Attribute Values	What the Attribute Does
`<a></a>` (anchor)	`href=`	[an absolute URL or a relative URL]	Specifies the link destination for a hyperlink.
	`name=`	[any string]	Creates a named anchor in a Web page.
	`target=`	[any string]	Activates a named browser window.
`<area>`	`coords=`	[two coordinate pairs for rectangles]	Specifies the location and size of a hotzone.
	`href=`	[an absolute URL or a relative URL]	Specifies the link destination for a hotzone.
	`shape=`	`RECT` for rectangles	Specifies the shape of the hotzone.
`<b></b>` (boldface)			
`<body></body>`	`background=`	[a filename]	Sets the background pattern for the page.
	`bgcolor=`	[a color name or hexadecimal color code]	Sets the background color for the page.
` `	`clear=`	`left` or `right`	Used in conjunction with images and tables (see Chapter Three).
`<dd></dd>` (deflist-definition)			
`<dl></dl>` (definition list)			
`<dt></dt>` (deflist-term)			

HTML Tags and Attributes

HTML Element	Attributes	Attribute Values	What the Attribute Does
`<em></em>` (emphasis)			
`<font></font>`	`face=`	[the name of a preinstalled type font]	Changes the typeface.
	`color=`	[a color name or hexadecimal color code]	Changes the text color.
	`size=`	n (an integer between 1 and 7) +n or −n	Changes the text size.
`<frame>`	`border=`	"N" (an integer)	Sets the width of the space around the frame in pixels. The default value is 5 pixels.
	`bordercolor=`	One of the 16 color names or a hexadecimal color code	Sets the color for one frame. (In some cases, it will set the border for a whole row or column.)
	`frameborder=`	"1" or "0"	Makes the borders around the frames sculpted (1) or not sculpted (0).
	`name=`	[string name]	Used to reference the frame from a `TARGET` attribute.
	`noresize`	[no value needed]	Prevents visitors from resizing the frame via drag-and-drop. The default allows resizing.
	`marginwidth=`	"N" (an integer)	Sets the distance (in pixels) between the left and right boundaries of a frame and its contents.
	`marginheight=`	"N" (an integer)	Sets the distance (in pixels) between the top and bottom boundaries of a frame and its contents.
	`scrolling=`	"YES", "NO", "AUTO"	Shows a scroll bar all the time (`YES`), never (`NO`), or only when needed (`AUTO`). The default is `AUTO`.

HTML Element	Attributes	Attribute Values	What the Attribute Does
	`src=`	[filename (relative or absolute)]	Inserts the specified file into the frame.
	`target=`	[string name signifying a frame (as set by the NAME attribute) or a browser window]	Sends the SRC file to the named location.
`<frameset> </frameset>`	`border=`	"N" (an integer)	Sets the width of the space between the frames in pixels. The default value is 5 pixels.
	`bordercolor=`	One of the 16 color names or a hexadecimal color code	Sets the colors for all frame borders in a frameset.
	`cols=`	"N" (an integer), "N%"(percentage), "*", or "N*"	Sets the width of the column in pixels, as a percentage of the available space or, in the case of an asterisk (*), whatever is left over from the other frames. N* divides the space among frames proportionally.
	`frameborder=`	"1" or "0"	Makes the borders around the frames sculpted (1) or not sculpted (0).
	`rows=`	"N" (an integer), "N%"(percentage), "*", or "N*"	Sets the height of the row in pixels, as a percentage of the available space, or whatever is left over from the other frames. N* divides the space among frames proportionally.
`<h1></h1>` (heading) `<h2></h2>` (heading) `<h3></h3>` (heading) `<h4></h4>` (heading) `<h5></h5>` (heading) `<h6></h6>` (heading)	`align=`	left, center, right	Justifies or centers the the heading. The default alignment is left justification.

HTML Element	Attributes	Attribute Values	What the Attribute Does
`<hr>`	`align=`	`left`, `center`, `right`	Justifies or centers the horizontal rule. The default alignment is centered.
	`noshade`	[takes no value]	Eliminates the default 3-D effect.
	`size=`	`n` (an integer)	Sets the thickness of the rule in pixels. The default size is 2 pixels.
	`width=`	`n` (an integer) or `n%`	An integer value sets the width of the horizontal rule in pixels. A percentage value sets the width as a percentage of the browser window's width. The default width is 100%.
`<i></i>` (italics)			
`<img>`	`align=`	`left`, `right`	Justifies the image against one side of the page with text flowing down alongside it.
	`alt=`	[a string of text]	Used by browsers that cannot display the image.
	`height=`	`n` (an integer)	Sets the height of the image in pixels.
	`src=`	[a filename]	Tells the browser which image file to display.
	`width=`	`n` (an integer)	Sets the width of the image in pixels.
`<li></li>` (list item)	`type=`	[any of the values associated with the `type` attribute for ordered lists]	Overrides any `type` attributes set by a relevant `OL` tag (applies only to ordered lists).

HTML Element	Attributes	Attribute Values	What the Attribute Does
	type=	[any of the values associated with the type attribute for unordered lists]	Overrides any type attributes set by a relevant UL tag (applies only to unordered lists).
	value=	n (a positive integer)	Indicates where to start counting (applies only to ordered lists).
<map></map>	name=	[any string]	Names the image map
<noframes></noframes>			For Web pages with frames, inserted just before the closing </frameset> tag. Insert the alternative content for browsers that don't support frames inside the NOFRAMES element.
<ol></ol> (ordered list)	type=	1	Labels list items with Arabic numerals (the default value).
		A	Labels list items with uppercase letters.
		a	Labels list items with lowercase letters.
		I	Labels list items with large Roman numerals.
		i	Labels list items with small Roman numerals.
	start=	n (a positive integer)	Indicates where to start counting.
<p></p> (paragraph)	align=	left, center, right	Justifies or centers the text and can also be used to

manipulate single lines of text.

<strong></strong>

HTML Element	Attributes	Attribute Values	What the Attribute Does
`<table>` `</table>`	`align=`	`left`, `right`	Justifies the table against one side of the page with text flowing alongside it. (*Note:* This attribute does *not* set the alignment for any cells within the table.)
	`bgcolor=`	[a color name or hexadecimal color code]	Sets the background color for all cells of the table (can be overridden by `TD BGCOLOR`).
	`border=`	n (an integer)	Sets the width in pixels of the beveled (3-D) border drawn around the entire table (the default value is 0). A non-0 border shows cell boundaries.
	`cellpadding=`	n (an integer)	Sets the width in pixels of a margin inserted inside the boundaries for each cell. (The default value is 2.)
	`cellspacing=`	n (an integer)	Sets the width in pixels of the boundary separating adjacent cells. (The default value is 2.)
	`summary=`	[a quoted string]	Summarizes the table for nonvisual browsers.
	`width=`	n (an integer), or n%	An integer value sets the width of the table in pixels. A percentage value sets the width as a percentage of the browser window's width.
`<td></td>` (table data) `<th></th>` (table headers)	`align=`	`left`, `center`, `right`	Sets the horizontal alignment for one cell. (The default value is `left`.)
	`bgcolor=`	[a color name or hexadecimal color code]	Sets the background color for one cell.
	`colspan=`	n (an integer)	Allows the cell to span n table columns.

HTML Element	Attributes	Attribute Values	What the Attribute Does
	nowrap	[takes no value]	Keeps all text inside the cell on a single line, unless explicitly broken with BR or P tags.
	rowspan=	n (an integer)	Allows the cell to span n table rows.
value	valign=	top, middle, bottom,	Sets the vertical alignment for one cell. (The default baseline is middle.)
	width=	n (an integer)	Sets the width of the cell in pixels.
<tr></tr> (table row)	align=	left, center, right	Sets the alignment attribute for each cell in one row (can be overridden by TD ALIGN).
	nowrap	[takes no value]	Disables line wrapping for all cells in the row.
	valign=	top, middle, bottom, baseline	Sets the vertical alignment for all cells in the row. (The default value is middle.)
<ul></ul> (unordered list)	type=	disc, circle, square	Changes the shape of the square bullet. The default value is disc.

APPENDIX D: SPECIAL CHARACTERS

Most of the keys on your computer keyboard will produce characters that browsers display "as is" after encountering them in a Web page. Other characters are special characters: they become visible on-screen only when you insert character codes in your Web page. All of the special characters listed in this appendix have numeric codes. Some also have symbolic codes, which are easier to remember. When both options are available, you can use either one. All special character codes begin with "&" (ampersand) and end with ";" (semicolon); be careful to include these delimiters whenever you insert a special character. The numeric codes must also include "#" (pound symbol) before the number. In addition, the symbolic codes are case-sensitive.

Special characters may be difficult to read in an `.html` file, but they work well when they are displayed by a browser. Always check your Web pages to confirm that they display any special characters correctly. The characters listed below are safe for use with any browser on any platform.

Character	Numerical Code	Symbolic Code	Character	Numerical Code	Symbolic Code
"	&#34;	&quot;	¥	&#165;	&yen;
"	&#147;		™	&#153;	
"	&#148;		©	&#169;	
#	&#35;		®	&#174;	
&	&#38;	&amp;	@	&#64;	
<	&#60;	&lt;	…	&#133;	
>	&#62;	&gt;	|	&#166;	&brkbar;
¬	&#172;	&not;	•	&#149;	
±	&#177;	&plusmn;	°	&#186;	&deg;
÷	&#247;	&divide;	§	&#167;	
µ	&#181;	&micro;	¶	&#182;	
¯	&#175;	&hibar;			
%	&#37;		à	&#224;	&agrave;
‰	&#137;		á	&#225;	&aacute;
¢	&#162;	&cent;	â	&#226;	&acirc;
$	&#36;		ã	&#227;	&atilde;
£	&#163;	&pound;	ä	&#228;	&auml;

Character	Numerical Code	Symbolic Code	Character	Numerical Code	Symbolic Code
å	&#229;	&aring;	ô	&#244;	&ocirc;
æ	&#230;	&aelig;	õ	&#245;	&otilde;
À	&#192;	&Agrave;	ö	&#246;	&ouml;
Á	&#193;	&Aacute;	ø	&#248;	&oslash;
Â	&#194;	&Acirc;	œ	&#156;	
Ã	&#195;	&Atilde;	Ò	&#210;	&Ograve;
Ä	&#196;	&Auml;	Ó	&#211;	&Oacute;
Å	&#197;	&Aring;	Ô	&#212;	&Ocirc;
Æ	&#198;	&Aelig;	Õ	&#213;	&Otilde;
è	&#232;	&egrave;	Ö	&#214;	&Ouml;
é	&#233;	&eacute;	Ø	&#216;	&Oslash;
ê	&#234;	&ecirc;	Œ	&#;	
ë	&#235;	&euml;	ù	&#249;	&ugrave;
È	&#200;	&Egrave;	ú	&#250;	&uacute;
É	&#201;	&Eacute;	û	&#251;	&ucirc;
Ê	&#202;	&Ecirc;	ü	&#252;	&uuml;
Ë	&#203;	&Euml;	Ù	&#217;	&Ugrave;
ì	&#236;	&igrave;	Ú	&#218;	&Uacute;
í	&#237;	&iacute;	Û	&#219;	&Ucirc;
î	&#238;	&icirc;	Ü	&#220;	&Uuml;
ï	&#239;	&iuml;	ÿ	&#225;	&yuml;
Ì	&#204;	&Igrave;	Ÿ	&#159;	
Í	&#205;	&Iacute;	ç	&#231;	&ccedil;
Î	&#206;	&Icirc;	Ç	&#199;	&Ccedil;
Ï	&#207;	&Iuml;	ß	&#223;	&szlig;
ò	&#242;	&ograve;	ñ	&#241;	&ntilde;
ó	&#243;	&oacute;	Ñ	&#209;	&Ntilde;

APPENDIX E: ANSWERS TO ODD-NUMBERED REVIEW QUESTIONS

Chapter One

1. HTTP is the universal communications protocol used by all Web servers and Web browsers. HTTP makes it possible for browsers to find Web pages using URLs.

3. A Web browser's cache is an area of the hard drive where the browser stores recently downloaded Web pages. If a user wants to revisit a page that's still in cache, the browser can retrieve its copy from the cache instead of going out to the Internet to download that page from the Web server. Retrieving files from caches saves time and bandwidth.

5. HTML, HEAD, TITLE, BODY

7. You can double-click on the file's archive, or you can go to the browser's File menu and select Open File or Open Page.

9. (1) Save the file with the Save command.
   (2) Load the file into the Web browser.
   (3) Review the Web page.
   (4) Revise the page as needed using a text editor or an HTML editor.
       (Go back to Step 1.)

Chapter Two

1. Headings (1) change the size of text, (2) change the text style to boldface, and (3) add blank lines before and after each heading.

3. Indentations are created by the HTML tags <ol>, <ul>, <dl>, and <block-quote>.

5. <dt> and <dd> work together inside a definition list (the <dl></dl> tag-pair).

7. (a) boldface or boldface;
   (b) italic or <i>italic</i>; (c) boldface italic or <i>boldface italic</i>

9. A <p> tag typically terminates a text line and inserts one blank line. A <br> tag terminates a text line, but does not insert any blank lines.

◎◎ Chapter Three

1. Hexadecimal color codes and RGB color codes.

3. BGCOLOR for solid colors and BACKGROUND for patterns.

5. The ALIGN attribute is used to make text flow around an image. You can set align="left" or align="right".

7. You scale an image by modifying its HEIGHT and WIDTH attributes. Reducing these attributes has no effect on the bandwidth requirements of the image.

9. You can preload images with the 1 × 1 pixel GIF trick.

◎◎ Chapter Four

1. The anchor element <a></a> uses the HREF attribute to create links.

3. This problem occurs when you forget to close an anchor element with the closing tag, </a>. To fix the problem, find the link label that was never closed and close it.

5. A portable Web site can be moved from one server to another with a minimal amount of work. Absolute links must always be updated when the target for the link changes location. Thus you can make your own site portable by avoiding absolute links to your own Web pages. Always use relative links to pages within your own site, and then preserve the directory structure from the original site when you move it to a new Web server.

7. The anchor element <a></a> uses the NAME attribute to create named anchors.

9. The only Web site that doesn't need ongoing link maintenance is a Web site that contains no (unavoidable) absolute URLs. If all of the URLs were relative URLs, the Web master would always know when a link required updating because he or she would control all of the target pages (and therefore know about any pages that move).

◎◎ Chapter Five

1. An adaptive color palette customizes its color selections for each image based on a frequency analysis of the colors in that particular image. The GIF file format supports an adaptive 256-color palette.

3. A progressive JPEG first displays a blurry version of its image early during a download process, then successively displays more details as the download progresses.

5. A transparent GIF is an image whose background behaves as if it were transparent when it is placed against the background color or pattern of the Web page. An interlaced GIF is an image that appears in stages while the image is downloading.

7. SHAPE, COORDS, HREF

9. Animated GIF files

◎◎ Chapter Six

1. The TR element organizes each table row, and the TD element organizes each table cell. TD elements go inside TR elements.

3.
```
<table cellpadding="10">
  <tr>
    <td bgcolor="red">
      text for the first column      </td>
    <td bgcolor="green">
      text for the second column      </td>
                                       </tr>
</table>
```

5.
```
<table>
  <tr>
    <td width="10" bgcolor="black">   </td>
    <td>
      <!-- the rest of the Web page goes here -->
                                       </td>
                                       </tr>
</table>
```

7.
```
<table width="100%">
  <tr>
    <td align="center">
      <!-- the IMG element goes here -->   </td>
                                       </tr>
</table>
```

9. The text in the next cell will not be red. The </TD> tag closes off any elements that are left open inside the current TD element.

◎◎ Chapter Seven

1. ROWS and COLS take fixed integers (for a pixel count), percentage values (to specify what percentage of the browser window should be allocated), and an asterisk (*) to allocate the browser window space remaining after all other frames have received their allocated space).

3. The FRAME elements are mapped to the regions determined in the FRAMESET tag in order, going from the upper-left corner of the window to the lower-right corner, one row at a time, moving through each row from left to right.

5. You must create two Web pages with FRAMESET elements and then nest one frameset inside the other. The top-level FRAMESET points to a displayable Web page as well as the other (inner) FRAMESET Web page. The inner frameset points to two displayable Web pages.

7. Deep linking is the practice of linking to a page at another site in a way that pulls the destination page out of its original intended context. U.S. courts have ruled that it is legal to link to a page at another Web site, even if that page is not the home page. If you link to a page at another site in a way that makes destination page appear to be your own, then you may be liable for damages.

9. Some people insist that no one should open a window on their computers without permission. Each new window consumes time (to close it) and computer resources. In particular, opening a new browser window can be annoying because the Back button returns the user only to the first page displayed inside that window. If too many browser windows are open, you may lose track of which one displayed the original page. It then becomes difficult to thread your way back to a Web page visited earlier in the session.

◎◎ Chapter Eight

1. A Web browser, a Web page construction kit, and an FTP client

3. `ftp://smith@elwood.student.univ.edu`

5. Yes; browsers can upload multiple files if you drag and drop a group of file icons into the browser's directory display.

7. If you share your computer with other users, you should not let the software save your password. If you do, others can access your Web site on the server.

9. You will see a "404 Not Found" error message in three instances: (1) you don't preserve your original directory structure when you upload files containing relative URLs; (2) the software you used to upload your files changed a filename (usually by changing the case of one or more characters); or (3) your Web pages contain URLs with the `file://` prefix.

INDEX

CREDITS

Figures 2.1, 2.3, 2.5, 2.6, 2.7, 3.1, 3.3, 3.4, 3.6, 3.7, 3.8, 3.9, 3.10, 3.11, 3.12, 4.2, 4.3, 4.5, 5.7, 5.9, 5.10, 5.14, 6.1, 6.3, 6.8, 6.10, 6.11, 6.13, 7.1, 7.2, 7.3, 7.4, 7.8	Netscape Communicator browser window © 1999 Netscape Communications Corporation. Used with permission. Netscape Communications has not authorized, sponsored, endorsed, or approved this publication and is not responsible for its content.
Figures 4.6, 4.7, 4.8	Used with permission from Viable Software Alternatives
Figure 5.4	From the `www.notes.net` article, "The Graphic Truth about Notes" by David DeJean
Figure 5.11	Collage Complete, a product of Inner Media, Inc. (`www.innermedia.com`)
Figure 5.12	email: uhfx@yahoo.com
Figure 8.8	Fetch Softworks